A MOMENT WITH GOD DEVOTIONAL BOOK

Dr. Travis S. Holmes

authorHOUSE®

AuthorHouse™
1663 Liberty Drive
Bloomington, IN 47403
www.authorhouse.com
Phone: 1 (800) 839-8640

Published by AuthorHouse 05/09/2016

ISBN: 978-1-5246-0847-7 (sc)
ISBN: 978-1-5246-0846-0 (e)

Library of Congress Control Number: 2016907648

Print information available on the last page.

Any people depicted in stock imagery provided by Thinkstock are models, and such images are being used for illustrative purposes only. Certain stock imagery © Thinkstock.

This book is printed on acid-free paper.

Because of the dynamic nature of the Internet, any web addresses or links contained in this book may have changed since publication and may no longer be valid. The views expressed in this work are solely those of the author and do not necessarily reflect the views of the publisher, and the publisher hereby disclaims any responsibility for them.

KJV
Scripture quotations marked KJV are from the Holy Bible, King James Version (Authorized Version). First published in 1611. Quoted from the KJV Classic Reference Bible, Copyright © 1983 by The Zondervan Corporation.

Dedication

This book has been written with a practical and simply understanding of the word of God. I have the honor and privilege of learning from one of God's anointed and finest preachers in this hour about blending both practical and theological in making it easy to grasp and gain wisdom from. A Moment with God is dedicated to my sister, pastor, and leader Dr. T.L. Penny the Presiding Prelate of Shubach World Cathedral in Sumter, South Carolina.

Underneath her wisdom, inspirational, and anointed teaching, preaching, and being an example of Holiness, I have learn to understand that this type of revelatory preaching and teaching that comes from spending quality time with the Lord. Through listening to her message, "*A Moment With God has birthed in my Spirit.*" God has instructed me to search the scripture and understand the real meaning through scriptural lessons and practical inspirations that "**God wants more of Him in us and less of us in us.**"

Dr. T.L. Penny had ministered a word to my soul through a message entitled, "*I am Jacob and this is my lump.*" Through receiving the nuggets from this message, it was striking, but revealing understanding that spending time with God is valuable and necessary for a believer to grow in the knowledge of God. Growing in the knowledge of God through spending quality time will leave evidence of a lump that you have spent that time with Him and Him with you.

As you read this book, I hope and pray that you will find a moment to spend with God and God with you that you may have a testimony that states, "*You have been with God and my evidence is my lump.*"

Preface

This book is written to help, shape, form, and foster a personal relationship with the Lord Jesus Christ. Through spending quality time with our Savior and Lord, it is how and why the believer growths and develops a personal solid, sound, and strong relationship. Relationships are built and develop from spending quality time with the person who you love the most. If a person truly loves God, He/she will spend that quality time with Him. Someone stated, "*Time is money and losing time is losing money*". The blessings will not flourish or multiply, unless the individual spending quality and meaningful time with the Lord and Savior Jesus Christ. The fact of the matter is that Lord Jesus Christ is *"The Blesser"* and a person should have a need, desire, and want to spend time with the one who blesses him/her.

Spending quality time with the Lord Jesus Christ is dedicating and committing to worship, prayer, and studying His word. It is not about reading or quoting scriptures, but mediating and fellowship with Him. Having *"A Moment with God"* is about spending a committed and dedicated time with the Lord Jesus Christ on a daily and consistence, continuous, and constant basis. Psalm 1:2, *"But his delight is in the law of the Lord; and in his law doth he mediate day and night"*. *"A Moment with God"* is about delighting, which indicates that a person must spend time, cleave, and commit to worship, prayer, and mediating on His word.

There is no secret to knowing, loving, and worshiping God, because these things happen when a person *"abide in Him and He abides in him/her"*. John 15:7, *"If ye abide in me, and my words abide in you, ye shall ask what ye will, and it shall be done unto you"*. The word abide mean to set up residence or dwelling in the midst of. Through spending *"A Moment with God"*, it is asking, requesting, and praying for the ultimate worship, fellowship, and praise to take course, which is the ultimate resolution of God dwelling in the midst of. This is when a person knows that God is doing more than listening and answering prayers, but He is actually dwelling within the person.

Hopefully, through this book *"A Moment with God Devotional Book"*, the individual will develop, learn, and gather principles and concepts of significance value for spending quality time with God that will develop and foster a productive and positive relationship that will yield results. This is my prayer and hope.

Week 1

I Should Heal Them

Matthew 13:15
*"For this people's heart is waxed gross, and their ears are dull of hearing,
and their eyes they have closed; lest at any time they should see with their eyes,
and hear with their ears, and should understand with their heart,
and should be converted, and I should heal them."*
(KJV)

The scripture above is indicating the solution for dissolving dull ears and waxed hearts. People hearts are waxed and ears dull, because wrong has invaded and gained territory in their hearts. The heart in this verse is a twofold connotation, which is a person's spirit or mind {**soul, will, emotion, or intellect**}. There are specific reasons why and how a person should keep one ears and hearts clean of wax and dullness.

Dull {**Wax**} is built up within a person, because one thing, which is called, {**sin**}. Sin is the core problem that causes the built up of wax and dullness within the individual. The scripture states, **"For this people's heart is waxed gross, and their ears are dull of hearing, and their eyes they have closed; lest at any time they should see with their eyes, and hear with their ears,."** There is no reason to allow sin to cause unnecessary issues that will limit a person ears from hearing and heart from receiving God's grace and mercy that will get rid of sin. The reason why sin needs to vacate the premises of a person lives for three reasons. The three reasons are understanding, conversion, and healing for others.

The 1ˢᵗ reason is understanding. Matthew 13:15, *"and should understand with their heart,"* The word understanding means to grasp the meaning of. There are some things that we will learn through experiences, but having experience does not necessary mean that we have learned anything. The key to measuring whether or not we have learned from our experiences is the ability to understand (grasp principles and precepts from the ordeal) and grow from it. The purpose for trails and tribulations is to execrated growth.

The 2ⁿᵈ reason is being converted. Matthew 13:15, *"and should be converted,"* The word converted means to change or transform. Through our experiences, change and transformation suppose to happen within us. The ultimate goal for walking with God is to know, understand, and notice that we are changing and we are not the same anymore. If we are the same individual when we accepted Jesus Christ, it is an indication that we have not accepted and received Him in our lives. The key to being converted is to notice real transformation from day to day.

The 3ʳᵈ reason is healing for others. Matthew 13:15, *"and I should heal them"*. The word heal means to cause (**an undesirable condition**) to be overcome. The Lord takes us through situations and circumstances that we may testify, preach, teach, and being example to show others that you can make it through. Our testimony, preaching, teaching, and living example are providing healing to those who are going through similar experiences and trails. Going through is for others to be heal from their ordeal, which comes from us being a living example on how to make it through.

In conclusion, it is important and essential to know, understand, and realize that our experience and transformations were done to help others along life's journey.

{Thought for the Week}
"Our experiences help others to heal."

Week 2

What You Need, God Got It! Pt-1

Hebrews 10:36
"For ye have need of patience, that,
after ye have done the will of God,
ye might receive the promise".
(KJV)

The scripture above is talking about the promises of God. God has promised all of us His guarantee blessings when we are obedient to His will. This is the key to knowing and understanding that God has what we need. God is always willing and able of supplying our needs, but we must know and believe that His promises are "**Yea and Amen**"! Knowing His promises will make us shout and dance with joy, because we know that God can't lie.

The first key is having patience. Hebrews 10:36, *"For ye have need of patience, that,"* The word patience means **not hasty, impetuous, able or willing to bear**. Patience is vital for grasping and waiting for the assurance of God's promises. The promises of God will come in do time, but we must have patience to wait on the Lord. This waiting on the Lord takes patience {**not hasty, impetuous, able or willing to bear**}, which means going through any and all situation knowing the outcome will be a blessing. We must have patience.

The second key is doing God's will. Hebrews 10:36, *"after ye have done the will of God,"* There are a lot of people who wants to be blessed {**receives His promises**} without being obedient to His will. The blessings of God come from being obedient to His will. For example, it is impossible to see the love of God working in our neighbor, if we hate our neighbor. The promises of God comes from putting the will of God into action, which is doing {**working, striving, and accomplishing**} His will.

The third and final key is receiving the promise. Hebrews 10:36, *"ye might receive the promise".* The word promise means to have agreement or contract between two individuals. God has a contract with us and we have with God when received Him as our personal Savior and Lord Jesus Christ. The truth is that we {**as being child of God**} sometimes beech our contract with God. Praise God for being God, because He is always merciful and patient with us and wait on us to come back to Him.

In conclusion, it is important and essential to note that God has what we need and He is willing to give us what we need.

{Thought for the Week}
"The Lord has what we need just be obedient to His promises."

Week 3

What You Need, God Got It! Pt-2

Philippians 4:19-20
*"But my God shall supply all your need according to his
riches in glory by Christ Jesus.
Now unto God and our Father be glory for ever and ever. Amen".*
(KJV)

It is important and essential to note that God is a provider. The word provider means to supply or make available. Jesus Christ knows how to supply and make available what we need. There is an ole adage that states, "**The Lord does not come when we want to, but He comes when we need Him**". This cliché states that God is a Provider.

A provider is likening to a father, grocery store, and anything or anyone who can provide a person with his/her basic needs. The Lord has already provides us with what we need, because He is a provider. He gives us health and strength, so we are able to do what we need to do in this life. The Lord knows how to look out for the need of the individual, which is food, shelter, clothing, and having good health.

<u>The first key is knowing that God is one who provide us with all our resources</u>. Philippians 4:19, *"But my God shall supply all your need according to his riches in glory by Christ Jesus"*. The word supply means to make available for use or satisfy. The purpose of God is to provide, which make resources available for us. But, the key is knowing that He is one that actually is the resource. The scripture teaches us that He is our Lord and Savior and we must know God for ourselves to know that He is a provider.

<u>The second key is knowing that all what God supplies is enough</u>. Philippians 4:19, *"But my God shall supply all your need according to his riches in glory by Christ Jesus"*. The phrase, "**supply all your need according to his riches in glory by Christ Jesus**". This phrase indicates that God gives enough and enough, so we want have to every need or want for nothing. I believe that God gives us everything we need from day to day, which the Bible called this "**our daily bread**". God gives us what we need everyday and it is enough.

<u>The third and final key is giving the Lord Jesus Christ thanks for what He has done</u>. Philippians 4:20, *"Now unto God and our Father be glory for ever and ever. Amen"*. This portion of the verse is indicating that God should be praised and worshiped for what He is and have already done. This is why Amen concluded this verse, because we should be in agreement with what God has already done and about to do for us. When we are coming into agreement with God, we are ***trusting, believing, and acknowledging*** Him to be a provider for us.

In conclusion, it is essential and imperative that a person get a personal relationship with God to know that God is a provider. A person must know the God of the resources to appreciate Him for providing those resources. What you need, God got it.

{Thought for the Week}
"The Lord always provides what we needs."

Week 4

What You Need, God Got It! Pt-3

Matthew 6:34
"Take therefore no thought for the morrow:
for the morrow shall take thought for the things of itself.
Sufficient unto the day is the evil thereof".
(KJV)

The scripture is above indicating a key solution for worrying. There is cliché that states, "**Why worry, if you are going to pray**?" When we know that the Lord had what we need, there is no reason to worry, be bothered, or scared. God has fixed and solved all our problems, but He wants us to believe and trust Him. Trusting and believing God is to key for receiving and knowing that He has what we need.

<u>The first key is not taking things in our own hands</u>. Matthew 6:34, *"Take therefore no thought for the morrow:"* There is nothing wrong with handling our business and making sure things are done, but this portion caution us to leave what we prayed for in the hands of God. There are some things that we can't change, but it is going to God to change. It is knowing and understanding when things are in our control and not in our control.

<u>The second key is not to over plan for tomorrow</u>. Matthew 6:34, *"for the morrow shall take thought for the things of itself."* The scripture is suggestion us not to be to caution and over plan. Planning is a key part of working out of our soul salvation, but our planning is stating that we are in charge and God is not leading us. When God is truly leading us, He wants us to plan, but give Him the opportunity to step in and provide guidance and provision. Remember, it is important not to over plan, but just plan and allow God to give the increase, provision, and leadership to our plans.

<u>The third and final key is understanding God provides what we need everyday</u>. Matthew 6:34, *"Sufficient unto the day is the evil thereof"*. The word sufficient implies that there is enough for this day. The Lord always gives us enough to make it through the day, but we must recognize and understand that He has already provided for us. The Lord already made things available for us, because He is a provider for His children. He is the Lord of our green pastures. He is the way maker to make a way out of no way. Praise the Lord, because He has provided for us everyday.

In conclusion, it is important to understand and grasp that God has what we need. He has what we need on today and forevermore. He is the same God yesterday, today, and forevermore, because He has what we need.

{Thought for the Week}
"The Lord gives us what we need everyday."

Week 5

When I Need Him Most

Psalm 27:10
*"When my father and my mother forsake me,
then the Lord will take me up".*
(KJV)

The above scripture indicates that the Lord is omnipresent at all times. Omnipresent means to be present everywhere at the same time. Proverbs 15:3, "**The eyes of the Lord are in every place, beholding the evil and the good**". (KJV) There is nothing or nowhere we can go and not be in the presence of the Lord. This is why we can reach out through worship and prayer and the Lord will come to our rescue.

The first key is understanding that Lord will never forsake me. Psalm 27:10, *"When my father and my mother forsake me,"* This portion of verse is discussed, because the importance of relying and depending on the Lord when the most important people in a person life forsake him/her. The word forsake mean to abandon, neglect, or dessert. **How do a person recover when your father or mother abandon or neglect you? Why is this statement important to person who have experience this outcome in his/her life?** It is important to realize and understand that God will never leave, abandon, or neglect us and we need to know that God is not like our nature born parents. He will always be there for us.

The second key is knowing that the Lord will be there. Psalm 27:10, *"then the Lord will take me up"*. The scripture is focusing on the nature attributes of the Lord, which is He is everywhere. The Lord will or can't be absent from a place or from a person life. He is there to provide, lead, guide, or counsel a person through an individual situation. A person must have a deep and penetrating relationship that must go beyond our situation and see that God is there.

The third and final key is trusting that the Lord is all a person needs. Psalm 27:10, *"then the Lord will take me up"*. The invisible text indicates to us that God is all we need. He is not just a provider, counselor, prince of peace, etc. He is all we need and can be anything for a person. I heard a preacher stated, "**God can be a substitute for anything in a person life, but there is no substitute for God**". He is all what a person needs.

In conclusion, the Lord knows how and why He steps in at the right time. He steps in a person situation, because He knows that a person needs Him. Whether or not a person acknowledges that he/she needs the Lord, the Lord always move on a person behave, because He knows that the person can't do anything without Him.

{Thought for the Week}
"The Lord steps in when we need Him the most."

Week 6

I Am Not Ashamed of Jesus Christ

Mark 8:38
*"Whosoever therefore shall be ashamed of me and
of my words in this adulterous and sinful generation;
of him also shall the Son of man be ashamed,
when he cometh in the glory of his Father with the holy angels".*
(KJV)

The scripture is taking about beginning and ending of the Christian Journey. The beginning of the Christian's journey begins with a person accepting Jesus Christ as his/her personal Savior. Then, the ending of the Christian's journey is when the same Jesus Christ who a person has accepted will come back to judge the living and the dead. The question will be asked, *"Did a person who accepted Jesus Christ was ashamed to acknowledge and proclaim Him before man?"*

In addition, it is essential and vital that he/she does not take one Christian Journey lightly. Taking one Christian journey lightly is what the church world call, *"**Playing Church**"*. Playing Church is phase that indicates that he/she does not have a relationship with Jesus Christ. Playing Church will ultimately catch and confront the individual at the judgment bar when Christ Jesus returns to judge the world. Just like Jesus Christ ascended into Heaven and He shall return the same way to judge this world.

The word ashamed comes from the root word shame, which means a painful sense of having done something wrong, improper, or immodest. Being a Christian is about having a character of love, honesty, truthfulness, and respectful. There are a lot of people who have the name of Christ Jesus banner on his/her shirt and bumper sticker, but never truly engaged in a real and meaningful relationship with Jesus Christ. When a person who been born-again, he/she will have a nagging conscience when he/she has wronged his/her neighbor. Here are five points for understanding not being ashamed (*a painful sense of having done something wrong, improper, or immodest*) of Jesus Christ.

<u>The first thing is having a relationship with Jesus Christ</u>. Mark 8:38, *"Whosoever therefore shall be ashamed of me"*

<u>The second thing is understanding the word of God</u>. Mark 8:38, *"Whosoever therefore shall be ashamed of me and of my words in this adulterous and sinful generation;*

<u>The third thing is not living according to this world</u>. Mark 8:38, *"Whosoever therefore shall be ashamed of me and of my words in this adulterous and sinful generation;"*

<u>The forth thing is knowing that the Lord will be ashamed to own us</u>. Mark 8:38, *"Whosoever therefore shall be ashamed of me and of my words in this adulterous and sinful generation; of him also shall the Son of man be ashamed,"*

The fifth and final thing is the denial of admittance in the present of His Father and Holy angels. Mark 8:38, "*when he cometh in the glory of his Father with the holy angels*".

In conclusion, it is essential to understand that being ashamed of Jesus Christ will cost a person at the judgment bar when seconding of the Lord Jesus Christ comes. It is important and essential that we must be real from the start, because starting wrong will have a wrong ending.

{Thought for the Week}
"If you are ashamed to lift up today,
He will be ashamed to honor you when He comes on tomorrow."

Week 7

Through the Valley of Baca

Psalm 84:6-8
"Who passing through the valley of Baca make it a well; the rain also filleth the pools.
They go from strength to strength, every one of them in Zion appeareth before God.
O Lord God of hosts, hear my prayer: give ear, O God of Jacob. Selah."
(KJV)

The scripture above indicates that there is a place called, "***The Valley of Baca***". The Valley of Baca is a place that has a meaning for "***weeping***". All of us as believers have our weeping moments are considered to be in a valley of trouble, pain, misery, or turmoil. Through these difference situations, a person will weep (***cry out***) to the Lord for help and strength. Today, a believer should be crying out to the Lord, because the condition of this world is very **self-centered, hateful, and deplorable** when comes down to treating each other according to the written word of God.

It is during a person "***Baca Experience***" that he/she will find strength and restoration. When a person weep, he/she is actually releasing whatever depress, misery, pain, or trouble one is battle from the inside to the outside. Baca is not necessarily a bad experience, but it is experience that all believers should and will have from time to time. Turmoil and pain will make anybody weep and turn to God for help and strength and "***Baca***" is a place to weep and find restoration for one's soul. There are five things a person will find in the "***Valley of Baca***."

The 1ˢᵗ thing is a place to be refreshed. Psalm 84:6, "*Who passing through the valley of Baca make it a well;*" A well is a place to get water (refresh oneself) from a lack of thirst. A person situation will cause him/her to thirst, but a place of weeping can turn to a place of being refreshed.

The 2ⁿᵈ thing is a place to be restored. Psalm 84:6, "*the rain also filleth the pools*". The word filleth means in scripture that something or someone had to be empty. When a person is empty, he/she is looking to be filled with God's grace and mercy to overflow his/her spirit. It is a place to find reconnection or recommitment to being regenerated with the Holy Spirit.

The 3ʳᵈ thing is a place to find strength. Psalm 84:7, "*They go from strength to strength,*" It is through a person weakness that he/she will find strength. Strength is untapped energy that comes from being in a place of weeping. When a person refused to weep anymore, he/she will find a reserve tank of strength to move from weeping to dancing.

The 4ᵗʰ thing is a place to worship. Psalm 84:7, "*every one of them in Zion appeareth before God*". The word "***Zion***" means the church. The church is a twofold meaning, which is an individual or specific location. Worship is developed and flourished through being in the Valley of Baca. Baca will put and place the individual in a place and position where he/she must worship the Lord.

The 5ᵗʰ and final thing is a place to get a prayer through. Psalm 84:8, "*O Lord God of hosts, hear my prayer: give ear, O God of Jacob. Selah*". Baca not only have a way of developing and fostering worship within the individual, but it has a way of developing and making a commitment to prayer. Prayer is a vital and necessary to know, feel, and believe in a God who can answer a person prayers. Prayers are answered, because a person went through the Valley of Baca.

In conclusion, the Valley of Baca is needed in a person lives, because it equips the individual with, so much of spiritual and natural growth that he/she need to experienced or received, if he/she didn't went through the Valley of Baca.

{Thought for the Week}
"The Valley of Baca is a place to experience."

Week 8

Count Your Blessings and See What the Lord had done!

Luke 2:20
"And the shepherds returned,
glorifying and praising God for all the things that they had heard and seen,
as it was told unto them".
(KJV)

The scripture above is indicating that a Christian should look and see what God is doing for him/her. There are some many things a person see and find what God has done and will do for the individual. It is important and essential to count and see what the Lord has done for a person to inspire and encourage one faith in him. Counting a person blessing is about appreciating and thanking God for what He has done and give a person understanding what the Lord will continue to do in a person future. Thanking and worshipping Him is essential and key ingredient for appreciating and thanking God for what He has done for a person.

The first key is leaders need be an example of let others know how good the Lord is. Luke 2:20, *"And the shepherds returned,"* The word shepherd is interrupted as pastor or leader of a flock. Leaders must have the ability and courage to inspirer and encourage others about His goodness. Fellowship is example of leadership in most situations. If the leader does not testify and praise God, it would be difficult to ask and inspire fellowship to do the same.

The second key is worship God for what you see and hear. Luke 2:20. *"glorifying and praising God for all the things that they had heard and seen,"* To really appreciate and thank God for what He has done is spending time worshipping Him. It is not about what God has done, but about who God is to the individual. When God is a person all and all, a person will continue to worship God at all times for all things He has done for the individual.

The third and final key is thanking God for keeping His promises. Luke 2:20. *"as it was told unto them".* The Lord is a God who doesn't and can't lie. He always keeps His promises. II Corinthians 1:20, *"For all the promises of God in him are yea, and in him Amen, unto the glory of God by us".* The Lord has indicated, which means He has promised His blessings for a person's life. It is essential that a person grasp and latch onto His promises.

In conclusion, the message is simply this. It is about entering into a position and place to worship and thank Him what he is doing and will do for us.

{Thought for the Week}
"Lord, help me to continue thank you for being a God that keeps your promises."

Week 9

Keep On Praying

Luke 18:1
*"And he spake a parable unto them to this end,
that men ought always to pray,
and not to faint:"*
(KJV)
I Thessalonians 5:17
"Pray without ceasing".
(KJV)

The scriptures above are talking about the importance of prayer. Prayer is how a person communicates with God and God communicates with him/her. Prayer is the individual tool and therapeutic mechanism to release and talk one's current and pressing issues. To neglect to pray, it is a lost opportunity to see the hand of God moving in a person's life.

Also, the scripture is indicating that a person should be persistent with one's prayer life. Persistent is the key to overcoming and prevailing over and through a person's situation. To overcome a current or future situation, the key is persistence. There is cliché in the collection finance business, which states, "***Persistence breaks Resistance***". A person must keep on praying and praying, until a break through comes. The word keeps mean to maintain or to carry on. A break through comes when a person continues to pray without ceasing, which is being persistence with a prayer life.

The 1ˢᵗ key is knowing that the Lord is in charge. Psalm 24:1, "*The earth is the Lord's and the fullness thereof; the world, and they that dwell therein*". Prayer is not only indicating to the Lord that a person can't do anything without His help and allowing Him to be in charge of a person current or pressing situation. When a person's pray, it is strong indication that he/she is submitting to authority of God to take control and be in charge of one's situation.

The 2ⁿᵈ key is knowing that prayer builds strength and keeps a person strong. Luke 18:1, "*that men ought always to pray and not to faint*". The word faint means to become powerless, weak, or feeble. A person becomes and gains power, strength, healing, and deliverance when an individual prays. The more a person's pray, the stronger a person gets. There is a cliché that states, "*Little prayer, little power. Much prayer, more power*". Prayer strength and build a person inner man, which is new man (new creature) within the individual. Prayer keeps a person strong and open communication with the Lord, which lead, guide, and direct a person into all truth and understanding.

The 3ʳᵈ and final key is keeping an inward prayer life. I Thessalonians 5:17, "*Pray without ceasing*". Prayer is an internal prayer life as well as a public prayer life. To pray without ceasing, a person must have internal and inward prayer life. An inward prayer life is "*pray without ceasing*", which is a consistent and constant prayer life going on within the individual. The word pray without ceasing is maintaining and carrying on continuous prayer life. A prayer life is something that is not just done in public, but it mostly done often and continuously in private, which is internal and inward prayer life.

In conclusion, it does not matter what and will come, but the key to surviving is continued to pray through the situation. It is important to keep on praying.

{Thought for the Week}
"Prayer is the key and faith will unlock the door."

Week 10

Just Say Thank You!

Psalm 106:1
"Praise ye the Lord.
O give thanks unto the Lord;
for he is good: for his mercy endureth for ever".
(KJV)

The scripture above is indicating and appreciating the Lord for who He is to person. A believer should know that the Lord is his/her all and all. When a person knows that He is one's everything, a person will being to appreciate Him with thanks and gratitude. The word thanks mean to show gratitude, appreciation, and honor to the Lord Jesus Christ. There are a lot ways to praise God, but a simple thank you Lord is always appreciative and appropriate.

The first thing is having a tendency to worship God more. Psalm 106:1, *"Praise ye the Lord"*. The more a person thinks about the goodness of Jesus Christ, a person will begin to praise God more and more, and thank God for what He has done. The worship is beginning and ending results of thanking the Lord for what God has done. It is through worship that a person begins to experience and see the goodness of God working in a person's life.

The second thing is having a humble and submissive attitude. Psalm 106:1, *"O give thanks unto the Lord;"* Being thankful is having a humble and submissive attitude so the Lord can exalt a person in due time. Reverend Eddie Salley Jr., which is my uncle stated, *"Be humble is key to being blessed by God"*. No one is blessed or give thanks when a person is unappreciative and not grateful.

The third thing is recognizing how good the Lord is. Psalm 106:1, *"for he is good:"* The word good means favorable or beneficial. When a person realizes how good the Lord is, it is indication that he/she is favored by God. The Lord favored those who are willing and obedient to His will. Being thankful is an indication that one recognized that God is good.

The fourth and final thing is knowing that God is merciful. Psalm 106:1, *"for his mercy endureth for ever"*. The word mercy means to have pity. God have pity on a person even when a person thinks that God is not having mercy. God have mercy on a person when a person thinks, act, and talk wrong and express things out of God's will. Mercy is withholding God's wrath and anger allowing His goodness, gentleness, and patience work for a person's favor.

In conclusion, it is important and essential that being thankful is the beginning of commune, fellowshipping, and adhering to God's instruction and will.

{Thought for the Week}
"A person should thank God for every little thing."

Week 11

I Learn How to Lean On the Lord

Proverbs 3:5-7
"Trust in the Lord with all thine heart;
and lean not unto thine own understanding.
In all thy ways acknowledge him,
and he shall direct thy paths.
Be not wise in thine own eyes:
fear the Lord, and depart from evil".
(KJV)

The Christian journey is about learning and understanding that all a person resource and source of life is in the Lord. Society teaches the opposite of relying and depending on the Lord, which is a gospel of humanism. The gospel of Humanism is a gospel that teaches and instructs an individual to cater to pleasing and depending on self. Psalm 14:1, *"The fool hath said in his heart, There is no God"*. A person becomes a fool when he/she thinks that he/she can only reply on self. To rely and depend on self, it is a boardline atheist disposition.

The scripture of above is teaching dependency. The word dependency means reliance or trust. Can a person learn to give up his/her independence to depend on the Lord? There is one thing that keeps a person from depending on the Lord, which is trust. Trust is a key component to faith, because one's faith is built and compacted by trust. If a relationship does not have trust, it will ultimately fail or dissolve with quickness.

This journey with the Lord is a faith walk and faith walk depends on having trust. Trust is only developed when a person spends quality time and the relationship has been tested to experience that teaches the person to trust God. Trusting God is a mindset that is driven by an inner strength. This inner strength is called, *"confidence"*. The more a person encountered situation and the Lord has worked things out in a person favor. The results will yield confidence that grows and grows to depend totally on the Lord. There are seven things that this particular scripture points out about Learning to Lean on the Lord.

The 1ˢᵗ thing is putting one trust in the Lord. Proverbs 3:5, *"Trust in the Lord with all thine heart;"*

The 2ⁿᵈ thing is not relying on self. Proverbs 3:5, *"and lean not unto thine own understanding."*

The 3ʳᵈ thing is acknowledging the Lord in everything. Proverbs 3:6, *"In all thy ways acknowledge him."*

The 4ᵗʰ thing is knowing the Lord keeps His promises. Proverbs 3:6, *"and he shall direct his paths"*.

The 5ᵗʰ thing is don't use your vision. Proverbs 3:7, *"Be not wise in thine own eyes;"*

The 6ᵗʰ thing is reverence God. Proverbs 3:7, *"fear the Lord,"*

<u>The 7th and final thing is turn from evil</u>. Proverbs 3:7, *"and depart from evil."*

In conclusion, learning how to lean and depend on the Lord will take three things. The three things are: *1) spending time with the Lord, 2) communicating with the Lord through prayer, and 3) having inner confidence to just trust the Lord.*

{Thought for the Week}
"A person path grows brighter day by day when he/she trusts God."

Week 12

The Word of Faith-Pt 1

Romans 10:8
"But what saith it? The word is nigh thee,
even in thy mouth,
and in thy heart: that is, the word of faith,
which we preach;"
(KJV)

The church has become a place where people come for a social gathering. A social gathering means to socialize about things in the world and what the world is doing or trying to do. The church should never be about a social gathering, but a place where an individual can receive a word of faith. The church is not just a local assembly, but people who are representation of the church. When the church becomes a social gathering, people who are looking for answers can't find a word of faith to inspire, encourage, and convince that Jesus Christ came to save them from all their sins.

However, there are movements within the church circle that states erroneous teaching about who is giving the word. Some preachers who proclaim the word have circulated a doctrine that is called, "**The right now word**". Preachers make statements, "**My word level is higher than next preacher word level**". This rhetoric makes people who are listening and hearing those preachers believe that preaching is about a profound and deep revelatory preaching that new twisted and dazzling understanding that has been created and discovered by their preaching. The scripture states, "**there is nothing new under the sun**", which implies a new, right now, or revelatory word is basically false doctrine.

People are flocking and being dazzled by this type preaching, because it is called, "**itching ears doctrine**". Itching ears doctrine does nothing for a person salvation and growth, because it puff up the soul with emotional soul mingling, which is "**mess**" that destroys the inner man and not built inner man faith. This type of stuff occurs, because people are not being taught to read, study, and mediate on "**The word of truth**". A personal relationship means not to wait for preacher to give a word of faith, but read, study, and mediate on the truths of God's word and preacher will come and confirm what God is speaking to individual.

Preaching the word of faith is not preaching about enquiring cars, houses, wealth, and status, but improving the relationship between man and God. The true preaching of the word of faith will teach and instruct people to seek God, His righteousness (**character, identity, and image**) and all those things (**houses, cars, wealth, and status**) will come from having a relationship with the Lord. Problem within the body of Christ, people are becoming more materialistic than spiritual minded, adhering, and submitting to leading of the Holy Spirit. The truth is that word inspire the Holy Spirit to fill the individual and Holy Spirit can only rule and guide, unless the word of faith is in the person heart.

In conclusion, it is essential and imperative that a person read, study, and mediate on the word of faith. The word of faith does not just come from the preacher on Sunday Morning, but through an individual personal devotional time with the Lord. Then, the word of faith will be **"nigh in thee"**.

{Thought for the Week}
"The word of faith is instructed, informed, and inspired the individual when a person take time to spend reading, studying, and mediating on the word of God."

Week 13

The Word of Faith-Pt 2

Romans 10:8
"But what saith it? The word is nigh thee,
even in thy mouth,
and in thy heart: that is, the word of faith,
which we preach;"
(KJV)

The word of faith is a word that has been used and misused within the church circle. People have used the word of faith to imply or give consent to have and do what a person wants to do at any given time. People have used faith in terms of *"naming it and claiming it"*. There are people naming and claiming a husband, but want go on a date with a man. There are people naming and claiming a house and car, but do not have a job to make payments on what they are naming and claiming. The word of faith has been misused, so people have gotten the misconception about what faith is really all about.

Faith is *trusting, believing, and knowing* that God can provide and do anything without reservation of doubt or unbelief. Faith is not just what God can do, but *believing, trusting, and knowing* source of the blessing(s), which is having a personal relationship with God and knowing He is the *"Author and Finisher"* of a person's faith. Faith is an act of obedience, which is derived from having a relationship with Lord Jesus Christ. The reality of faith is being obedient to God and following His will and purpose God has for the individual.

The 1ˢᵗ thing is understanding the word of faith. Romans 10:8, *"But what saith it?"* It is important and essential that a person seeks to understand faith. Faith derives from having a relationship with God and God with the individual. Understanding is the key to utilizing and demonstrating *"faith properly and maturely"* without delusional misconception.

The 2ⁿᵈ thing is knowing the word suppose to be in a person's mouth and heart. Romans 10:8, *"The word is nigh thee, even in thy mouth and in thy heart:"* A person who has a relationship with Lord will display and demonstrate a confession that speaks faith that comes from heart and links out a person's mouth. Speaking faith only can come from having the word in one's mouth and heart, which is derived from mediating, reading, and studying the word.

The 3ʳᵈ and final thing is accepting and receiving the preach word of faith. Romans 10:8, *"that is, the word of faith, which we preach,"* The word preach means to proclaim or make an announcement. The preach word is announcement of faith in who and what God can do. When a person receives the preach word of faith, he/she is able to accomplish and see clearly what God's plan, purpose, and promises are for his/her life.

In conclusion, the word of faith is literally taking the word and applying it to a person's life. Reverend Eddie W. Salley Jr., which is my uncle and pastor when I was little boy had stated,

"Once you have heard the word, you must apply the word. Hearing the word is no good, if you don't apply it to your life."

{Thought for the Week}
"Hearing the word is no good, if you don't apply, it to your life."

Week 14

The Word of Truth-Pt. 1

II Timothy 2:15
"Study to shew thyself approved with God,
a workman that needeth not to be ashamed,
rightly dividing the word of truth."
(KJV)

The truth is what most people are looking even when people does not want accept or receive it at that particular time. No one wants anyone to lie or mislead them, because everyone wants the truth. The question is, *"How much of the truth can a person accept and receive?"* This question is probably answered, because *80%* of those who attend church from Sunday to Sunday does not study or read the Bible on a daily bases. This is a stocking and alarming percentage, because this percentage states that people who come to church is just hearers and not those who are willing to learn and grasp the principle truths of God's word. To learn and grasp the principle truths of God's word, it will take quality time with the Lord.

The scripture above indicates that the Bible is the word of truth. The only way to learn and understand the word of truth is to study the word of the truth. The word study means to read in *detail, mediate, reflect, or consider attentively*. To understand and embrace the word of truth, it is going to take careful examining (*considering attentively*) what the word is declaring to the individual. The word of truth is bringing clarity and understanding, so a person can declare truth to his/her life.

The 1ˢᵗ thing is the word of truth brings understanding about God. II Timothy 2:15, *"Study to shew thyself approved with God,"* The purpose for studying the word of truth is for learning about God. When a person learns about God, it is *"bridging and fostering"* a personal relationship with God and God with him.

The 2ⁿᵈ thing is the word of truth helps the person to improve. II Timothy 2:15, *"Study to shew thyself approved with God;"* The word of truth helps the individual to get better and better from day to day. When a person knows better, he/she will ultimately and usually *"do better"*.

The 3ʳᵈ thing is the word of truth assures that individual will not be ashamed. II Timothy 2:15, *"a workman that needeth not to be ashamed,"* Knowing the word of truth, it will eliminates and keeps a person from *"falling and enduring"* unnecessary hardship and pain. The truth will make a person see clearly what is going on.

The 4ᵗʰ and final thing is the word of truth should be stated clearly and correctly. II Timothy 2:15, *"rightly dividing the word of truth."* The phase *"rightly dividing the word of truth"* means to correctly and factually proclaim the truth. The truth should be told in the simplest terms were a new born baby can understand what is going on.

In conclusion, the word of truth is indicating the true meaning and purpose of having a relationship with Jesus Christ were others can see what God can do within the individual.

{Thought for the Week}
"The truth should be told in the simplest terms were a
New-Born baby can understand what is going on."

Week 15

The Knowledge of the Truth

I Timothy 2:3-4
"For this is good and acceptable in the sight of God our Savior;
Who will have all men to be saved,
and to come unto the knowledge of the truth."
(KJV)

The scripture above is talking about salvation. Salvation is when a person has repented and accepted Jesus Christ as one personal Savior. Through repenting and accepting Jesus Christ, the person is stating that he/she has acknowledged and recognized the truth of Salvation. The truth about salvation is, ***"accepting, believing, and receiving"*** Jesus Christ as a person's Lord and Savior. The obvious truth about this statement is acknowledging the fact without Jesus Christ being a person's Lord and Savior that he/she will be lost and on the way to a devil's hell.

The important of this verse is ***"to come unto the knowledge of the truth."*** The word knowledge means to be made known or discover reality. When a person receives knowledge, he/she is more aware of his/her condition. The knowledge of the truth will support and encourage the idea of embracing change. **Reason why** ***"the knowledge of the truth"*** **embraces change, because a person must** ***"come unto the truth of knowledge"*****,** which is embracing and receiving, the idea of hope and opportunity to change.

As a result, the knowledge of the truth will embrace the truth of God's mercy and grace. God's mercy and grace is that ***"who will have all men to be saved"*****. The Lord Jesus Christ desire and hope is that** ***"all men to be saved"*****.** The word saved means to be delivered or rescued from sin and the penalty of sin. Through providing the opportunity to come unto the knowledge of truth, there is no excuse for receiving the eternal hope of glory, which accepting and receiving Jesus Christ as one personal Savior and Lord.

Therefore, the knowledge of truth must be preached and taught to all people no matter whether or not he/she accepts the knowledge of truth. The intrinsic truth about the word of God is no one will go to hell for not hearing and knowing that God has revealed and spoken the knowledge of the truth to him/her. The knowledge of the truth is very powerful and acceptable that it is pleasing to God. The **scripture states, *"For this is good and acceptable in the sight of God our Savior;"*** which is accepting and receiving the knowledge of the truth.

In conclusion, it is vital and necessary that person understand that he/she must accept and receive the knowledge of the truth. The scripture is states, ***"the truth"*****,** which implies not to receive no one else view, perspective, or idea of the truth. The only truth that a person needs to believe, accept, and receive is ***"the knowledge of the truth"***, which is declared and founded in the word of God-The Bible.

{Thought for the Week}
"It is important not to receive no one else view, perspective, or idea of the truth."

Week 16

Peace Be Within Thee

Psalm 122:7-8
"Peace be within thy walls, and prosperity within thy palaces.
For my brethren and companions' sakes,
I will now say, Peace be within thee."
(KJV)

The scripture above is talking about value and importance of peace. Peace is the results of having the living Savior Jesus Christ abiding on the inside of individual. No one can deny the power of peace, because peace is one the attributes of having the power of the Holy Spirit abiding and dwelling within and characteristic of the fruit of Jesus Christ. The fruit of Jesus Christ is having the mind and heart of God, which the devil is denounce and God is evaluated within the heart of the individual.

Therefore, peace rules the heart and mind individual, which peace abiding and through the individual changes the atmosphere and environment where the individual resides. The scripture states, **"Peace be within thy walls,"** and walls are indicating the palace (**where individual resides**). There is no place like home and a person should always find peace abiding within the walls of his/her home. The promise that God gives an individual that peace will govern a person's life.

In addition, the result of peace is prosperity lives within the walls of the individual home. The scripture states, **"and prosperity within thy palaces"**, which is the hallmark for abiding, dwelling, and allowing the Holy Spirit to lead and govern a person's life. There is a lot of erroneous teaching and preaching that indicates prosperity is equated to having material wealth. The true measuring tool for having these things is having peace dwelling within and palace (**where individual's resides**) is filled of tranquility. A person may have a lot of material possess, but his/her inner self and home can filled with activity and den that is filled with strife and turmoil.

When a person has peace, it is to enhance and strengthen each other. The scripture states, **"For my brethren and companions' sakes,"** which indicates that peace is there help my fellowman. Peace is to be shared and felt by others. People love to be around a person who life is filled with tranquility and present is delightful and pleasant to be in and around. The truth of matter is peace comes from having Holy Spirit and the Holy Spirit is the agent of peace.

Finally, the reason why a person is engulfed and regenerated with peace, because he/she has been born-again and filled with the Holy Spirit. No one can make and create an atmosphere of peace, unless God is governing, abiding, and residing in person. The scripture states, *"I will say,*

Peace be within thee." This is a statement of declaration and promise. When a person truly repents and turns to God, He is reasons why peace is within the individual.

{Thought for the Week}
**"The true attributes of having Jesus Christ is turmoil and misery is removed
and replaced with His peace within the heart and mind of the individual."**

Week 17

The Word of Truth-Pt. 2

John 17:17
"Sanctify them through thy truth:
thy word is truth."
(KJV)

The church is an individual who have been called **"out of darkness into the marvelous light of salvation"**. The true definition of church, which is the **born-again, baptized, and filled with the Holy Spirit believer.** There is a lot of erroneous teaching that relates to what is the church. The church is called sometimes **"sanctify or holiness church."** If a person church or individual are not apart of so-called sanctify or holiness church, the church or individual is considered not to be a true church. This is not founded in the word of truth.

The word of truth is about speaking, sharing, and witnessing the truth of God's word. The words **sanctify and holiness** is related to the way a person should live his/her life. Holiness and sanctification is not a specific domination, but attribute of the characteristics of having Jesus Christ living and abiding within the person's life. The church, **whether it is a person or location should be separated from evil and set apart to be used by God.** This is the true meaning of sanctification and holiness teaching as it relates to the word of truth, which is accepting Jesus Christ and denouncing and coming out of sin.

The preacher is held accountable to a higher standard, because he/she suppose to be preaching, teaching, and being able be a living example of **"The word of truth."** The Word is found in the Bible. When a preacher detours for the word, he/she will usually begin to make stuff up. Making stuff up is called, **"The doctrine of men."** The truth is man's doctrines that will ultimate leads a person to a devil's hell that was made for the devil and his fallen angels. This truth is actually called, **"The blind leading the blind and both will fall into the ditch."**

It is critical and imperative that word is being taught from its pure, real, and practical applicable point of view, so all can grasp the simple truths of God's word. If there is teaching and preaching on sanctification, it should be taught from the word at its pure and real since of the word. No one can argue or deny the truth when it is clearly and understandably exampled from the word of God. Everybody and anybody are looking for truth and truth is certainly comes from **"The Word"**, because **"Thy word is truth."**

In conclusion, a person can only be sanctified by the word. Joining a local assembly under the banner of sanctification does not make a person sanctify, because it is just a word that displays on the church billboard. A person becomes sanctify when he/she believes, accepts, and receives

Jesus Christ as personal Savior. This is how a person is ***"sanctify by the truth"***, which is the word of truth.

{Thought for the Week}
"True sanctification comes from accepting and receiving Jesus Christ
as an individual personal Savior and Lord."

Week 18

The Importance of Worship

John 4:24
*"God is a Spirit: and they that worship him must
worship him in spirit and in truth."*
(KJV)

The importance of worship is about a person having a relationship with God and God with him. A relationship with the Lord Jesus Christ depends on a person accepting, believing and receiving Jesus Christ as one's Savior. Worship brings out the true and real meaning of salvation, which is appreciation and gratitude of being saved from one's sin. If being saved from sin and penalty of sin, which death does not make an individual worship God. What will make a person's magnify and lift up the name of Jesus Christ?

The essence of worship is depending upon worshipping God in the Spirit, because God can only be worship in the Spirit. The scripture states, *"God is a Spirit:"* The only way to reach God through mediator Jesus Christ is through being filled and baptized in the Holy Spirit. To reach God in the Spirit, a person must have the Holy Spirit and *"not a spirit,"* because God the Father, Jesus Christ the Son and the Holy Spirit is *"one."* Ephesians 4:5, *"One Lord, One Faith, One baptism."* Worship depends upon a person having the Holy Spirit and the Holy Spirit must be in the person.

As a result, the church circle have adopted a cliché that states, *"in spirit"* or *"catching the Holy Ghost"* (Holy Spirit), which the Holy Spirit and Holy Ghost is same and have the same meaning. The scripture states, *"and they that worship him must worship him in spirit and in truth."* Being *"in the spirit or catching the Holy Spirit"* does not mean that a person necessary must *dance, cry, or scream* from tip of his/her lungs. Being *"in spirit"* or *"catching the spirit"* should be centered and focused on a person willing to yield and submit to Holy Spirit to lead, guide, teach, and counsel the individual. When the Holy Spirit moves on the altar of an individual heart, he/she transformed and changed to follow the will of God.

Also, the importance of worship is about three core principles. **The core principles are: 1) fellowship, 2) Commune (intimacy), and 3) authentic spirit.** It is near impossible to worship God with false heart, because falsity does not move the altars of God's heart. God's heart is moved and quickened by being *"in spirit and in truth."* The scripture states, *"and they that worship him must worship him in spirit and in truth."* The only way to move God, a person *"must worship him in spirit and in truth."* The word must is key, because it indicates there is no other way, but the right way. The right way is *"worship him in spirit and in truth."*

In conclusion, the importance of worship goes beyond dancing, screaming, and shouting from the tip of a person's lungs. The importance of worship is about having a real, truthful, and meaningful relationship with Jesus Christ. Worship only begins when a person has repented, accepted and received Jesus Christ as Lord and Savior.

{Thought of the Week}
"The importance of worship starts when a person
has repented, accepted, and received Jesus Christ as Lord and Savior."

Week 19

I Told You, You Will See Me Again

Matthew 27:63
"Saying, Sir, We remember that that deceiver said,
while he was yet alive,
After three days I will rise again."
(KJV)

In the above scripture, it is talking about Jesus Christ being crucified and resurrected. The gospel of Jesus Christ main focus and source validity hangs on the **death, burial, and resurrection.** Without the resurrection of Jesus Christ, there is no gospel. Without the resurrection of Jesus Christ, there is no victory to claim and receive. The resurrection is pivotal focal point of the gospel, which is the good news of Jesus Christ.

However, the scripture within this verse reveals a promise that Jesus Christ has made. A promise is contractual agreement between two or more parties. When the Lord Jesus Christ makes a promise, He always fulfills His promises. II Corinthians 1:20, *"For all the promises of God in him are yea, and in him Amen, unto the glory of God by us."* All of His promises are yes and Amen, which implies that God always fulfill His word.

There are some people who do not keep there promises. Pastors are bad examples at times when comes to keeping promises. A Pastor will tell a member that **"I am coming by to see you or I will pray for you, and sometimes the Pastor forget to do both."** My recommendation is to following Jesus Christ examples, which is always do what we say we are going to do. Promises are so easily to break, because a person sometime makes those promises with God intention, but fail to fulfill those promises.

But, the scripture above is indicating a powerful truth about Jesus Christ commitment to the believer and sinner. The scripture stated, *"After three days I will rise again."* The Lord Jesus Christ made a promise to the believer that He will never leave or forsake him/her. In same statement, He made a promise to the sinner that He will save, deliver, and loose him/her from the bondage of sin. Romans 5:8, *"But God commendeth his love toward us, in that, while we were yet sinners, Christ died for us."* Jesus Christ made a commitment to free the sinner from sin and strengthen the believer to run on in His name.

In conclusion, it is extremely important that Lord Jesus Christ always keep His promises. Remember, He told us that we will see Him again.

{Thought for the Week}
"The Lord always keeps His promises."

Week 20

Loving People the Right Way

I John 3:16-20
"Hereby perceive we the love of God, because he laid down his life for us:
and we ought to lay down our lives for the brethren.
But whoso hath this world's good, and seeth his brother have need,
and shutteth up his bowels of compassion from him, how dwelleth the love of God in him?
My little children, let us not love in word, neither in tongue; but in deed and in truth.
And hereby we know that we are of the truth, and shall assure our hearts before him.
For if our heart condemn us, God is greater than our heart, and knoweth all things."
(KJV)

There is a cliché that states, **"Love is not what a person say, but what it does."** Reverend Eddie W. Salley Jr. has been preaching for years and years. He stated in many of his sermons that love is the key to making it into heaven. Heaven is made for prepared people and God's people are prepared to enter into heaven by love. Love is the epitome of Jesus Christ, because He died and rose again by love.

Love is an action word, which means a person must show love and not just talk love. There is a cliché that states, **"Let us not talk the talk, but walk the walk."** The word love means to have a continuous of cherishing, devoting, and taking pleasure in it. **The hallmark for a *strong, true, real, and genuine relationship* with Lord and with others is love**. The way a person love people has everything to do with whether or not a person has a relationship with Jesus Christ.

The three principles of loving people are: *1) Cherishing, 2) Devote, and 3) Take Pleasure*. The word *cherishing* means whether or not a person value the relationship, because value will tell a person how far a person is willing to go. The word *devotes* means to spend quality time with the one the person loves. The word *take pleasure* means to enjoy spending time with the person you love. The message is clear about how and why a person should treat, relate, and greet each other. Love is the principle key ingredient for using a measuring tool to reach out to others. There are five key principles for reaching out to others. These three principles are:

<u>*The 1st thing is Jesus Christ is the example on how to display love.*</u> **(ver. 16)**
<u>*The 2nd thing is love not neglecting each other needs.*</u> **(ver. 17)**
<u>*The 3rd thing is putting love into action with sincerity.*</u> **(ver. 18)**
<u>*The 4th thing is love will put assurance in our worship.*</u> **(ver. 19)**
<u>*The 5th and final thing is love find out where you are in regards to your relationship with people.*</u> **(ver. 20)**

The truth about loving people comes from having an intimate relationship with the Lord Jesus Christ. The way a person treats and handles people from day to day is reflection of having or not having a relationship with God. The reason why this is true, because God is love and reason why a person has his/her ability, talent, strength, mind, and heart to have a desire, need, and want to love others. God is love and love comes from God.

In conclusion, the primary key reason for loving people the right way is from having a real, genuine, and sincere relationship with the Lord Jesus Christ.

{Thought for the Week}
"Loving others is extension of having a real, genuine, and
sincere relationship with the Lord Jesus Christ."

Week 21

Go Ye Therefore!

Matthew 28:19-20
"Go ye therefore, and teach all nations,
baptizing them in the name of the Father, and of the Son, and of the Holy Ghost:
Teaching them to observe all things whatever I have commanded you:
and, lo, I am with you always, even unto the end of the world. Amen."
(KJV)

The above scripture talks about fulfilling and accomplishing God's mission in this world. The word mission means to accomplish a task or fulfill a certain assignment. The Lord Jesus Christ has commissioned the church to be community based and centered. To be community based and centered means all programs and services are geared to serve the community. The church is not about servicing those who are saved, but geared to reaching the lost.

The church is called "***the called out ones.***" The called out ones are those who are saved and filled with the Holy Spirit, which is a phase that the church uses-"***being born-again.***" The church should be those who are "***born of the spirit and water.***" This phase means a change must come within the individual from accepting and receiving in Jesus Christ as his/her personal Savior and Lord. No one is saved and received Jesus Christ except from having someone given the invitation to Christ Jesus. The invitation comes from having someone "**introduce and invite**" a person to Jesus Christ.

Therefore, the church is about going into the world and ministering the gospel of Jesus Christ to the lost. The scripture states, "***Go ye therefore, and teach all nations,***". The word "***go***" means "***to be called to something, someone, or somewhere.***" When a person goes into the world, he/she is commissioned to teach. The word teach mean to instruct or show a person what the word is saying. Reason why church has became dominant in this century, because no one can be commissioned to the world, because he/she has not being instructed to "***go.***"

The possible of reaching the lost comes from a person being energized and being filled with the Holy Spirit. The scripture states, "***baptizing them in the name of the Father, and of the Son, and of the Holy Ghost:***" A believer be energized and fueled by the Holy Ghost to do God's word, will, and way. The word will work when a person is doing His will and way. No one can say that drawing others to Jesus Christ comes from just sitting in the church. The church (***the born-again believer who are filled with the Holy Ghost***) must "***go***" and do God's will through leading, guiding, and directing from the Holy Ghost. The Holy Ghost will lead and guide a person to minister the word of the Lord to the lost.

In conclusion, the purpose of going is the minister to the lost and knowing that God will always be with the individual. The scripture states, "***and, lo, I am with you always, even unto***

the end of the world. Amen." God wants a person to reach, rescue, and restore the lost through the church going out into the world and ministering to those who are lost.

{Thought for the Week}
"Go and Reach the lost at any cost."

Week 22

I Will

Jeremiah 30:17
"For I will restore health unto thee, and I will heal the of thy wounds,
saith the Lord; because they called thee an Outcast, saying,
This is Zion, whom no man seeketh after."
(KJV)

The scripture above is indicating a commitment that the Lord has with His children. A commitment is nothing, but a *"**Promise, Contract, or Mutual Agreement.**"* The phase *"**I Will**"* is mention twice in the verse above. This is indicating that the Lord is placing emphasis on His promise to the believer. The idea is to encourage and give assurance to the believer that God has made His promise and He will keep His promised to those who *"**Trust, Believe, and Accept**"* His will for his/her life.

However, the scripture is directly conversing about salvation. Salvation does more than helping and strengthening a person in the spiritual realm. Salvation brings healing and restoration to whole man. Restoration and Healing is done twofold once a person receives salvation. The twofold emphasis in the scripture above is talking about healing for soul and body. It is ironic to know and understand that there are many types of healing. There is healing for the mind, body, emotion, finance, spirit and etc. To really understand this promise, the Lord has made a promise to heal a person body internally and externally.

The 1st thing is that God has promised to heal a person body. Jeremiah 30:17, *"For I will restore health unto thee,"* The word health is indicating that it is directly talking about a person body. The key to understanding point of salvation is that God came to *"restore health"* back to the individual. There is no mistake about salvation, because salvation heals the whole man both body, soul, and spirit.

The 2nd thing is that God has promised to heal a person wounds. Jeremiah 30:17, *"and I will heal the of thy wounds, saith the Lord;"* The word wounds mean emotion and psychological that have directly deals with the soul. There are some things that have *"cut at the core of a person's life"* that he/she never recovered from those wounds. Wounds are not cuts, because cuts are just scratching the surface, but wounds cut deep and below the surface of a cut. The salvation seeks to heal what is below the surface of the cut.

The 3rd and final thing is that has promised to preserve Zion. Jeremiah 30:17, *"because they called thee an Outcast, saying, This is Zion, whom no man seeketh after."* The scripture indicates, *"This is Zion,"* which means the church (**the local assembly or the body of Christ**). The word *"**Zion**"* is representation of the church and the church suppose to be a place and individual that representation of the love making a person whole through having and receiving salvation. The promise is that God will not allow His church to be a castaway.

In conclusion, it is important to realize, understand, and acknowledge that fact the God always keep His promises. But, the key is to "*believe, accept, and receive His promises to yield and manifest*" in the individual lives. The person must know that "*I will*" means that the Lord always keep His promises.

{Thoughts for the Week}
"The Lord always keeps His promises."

Week 23

The Essence of Salvation

Ephesians 4:24
"And that ye put on the new man,
which after God is created in righteousness and true holiness."
(KJV)

The above scripture is talking about the essence of salvation. The essence of salvation means the very plan and purpose for salvation. Please understand and know that salvation means to be saved from sin and the penalty of sin, which is death. The Essence of Salvation is rescue, restore, and revive the soul of the individual through transformation into a new man, which was brought and made available through accepting, believing, and receiving Jesus Christ as one Lord and Savior. Jesus Christ is reason why and how salvation became, so ***important, valuable, and significant*** to the individual.

The verse talks about *"And that ye put on the new man,"* which is indicating that one must be born-again or transformed into a new person. The phase *"put on the new man"* means to actually making a commitment to surrender, submit, and serve God's will. To put on requires a definite action, because salvation just does not happen overnight or a person guess or scratch off a lobby ticket and become save. The scripture is indicating that *"put on the new man"* is a required action, which is result from ***accepting, believing, and receiving Jesus Christ as Lord and Savior***.

However, salvation is a ***constant, consistent, and continuous*** working progress that individual should do on a daily basis. A working progress is described in two categories, which are *"righteousness and true holiness."* The working progress begins after a person is created new in God. The scripture states, *"which after God is created in righteousness and true holiness."* To be created means to be shape, mold, or form. When a person accepts and receives Jesus Christ, there is a shaping, molding, and forming that is done within the individual. This is called, *"which after God is created in righteousness and true holiness."*

The working progress begins in two areas, which are righteousness and true holiness. This portion talks about the working progress beginning *"in righteousness and in true holiness."* **The 1ˢᵗ area** is *"in righteousness."* The words *"in righteousness"* mean that a person must have a relationship with the Lord Jesus Christ and the Lord Jesus Christ must have a relationship with Him. Through this relationship with the Lord Jesus Christ, a standard will begin to rise within the individual. The word righteousness actually means to have a standard or live by certain principles and guidelines.

Also, **the 2ⁿᵈ area** is *"in true holiness."* The word holiness means to live a holy (*complete or mature lifestyle*), which is only derived from having a personal relationship with the Lord Jesus Christ. The words *"true holiness"* indicates that an individual must ***be real, genuine, and sincere*** about living right before a Holy God. The Lord Jesus Christ requires a person to be holy, because he/she is worshiping and serving a Holy God.

In conclusion, the essence of salvation is accepting and receiving Jesus Christ as Lord and Savior, which is the important, valuable, and significant to a person salvation.

{Thought for the Week}
"Salvation is a constant, consistent, and continuous working progress."

Week 24

Lord Will Fix It

Psalm 57:7
"My heart is fixed, O God, my heart is fixed;
I will sing and give praise."
(KJV)

The true value of salvation is hanging on the hinges of knowing, believing, and trusting God to fix things. A person's faith is totally placed and positioned in depending totally on the Lord Almighty. The reason why a person is committed to **serving, worshiping, and praising God**, because he/she believes that the Lord is able to do anything, but fail. Failure is not in Lord Almighty category, because there is no failure in God.

The word fixed means to repair what is broken. This is a truthful and meaningful word in this verse, because the word fixed is mention twice. When a word is mention more than once in a verse, it means this is personal and has significant meaning. The Lord Jesus Christ specializes in "**healing, strengthening, and repairing**" what was and is broken within an individual.

The Bible declares that psalmist stated twice that God has fixed his heart. The emphasis is on "**My heart**", which indicates it is a personal testimony. There are some things that no one will ever know or see what God has done for a person. There is song that states, "**You wasn't there and don't know how, what God has done for me.**" The statement "**my heart is fixed**" is mention twice, which gives more meaning and powerful for the individual.

After the Lord fixes a person heart, there is an action a person's makes. When the Lord Jesus Christ fixes a person's situation, a person can "**believe, know, and see**" what God can do. The situation (**fixing a person's heart**) usually prompts an action from the individual to commit to the Lord Jesus Christ. The Lord makes a way for a person and a person should commit to serving and doing His will, because what the Lord has done for a person.

The scripture states, "**I will**" means to there is a commit to the Lord. When the Lord really moved and fixed things in a person's life, he/she will do two things. **The 1ˢᵗ thing is "I will sing"**, which is indication of giving a testimony for what God has done for the individual. **The 2ⁿᵈ and final thing is "I will give praise"**, which is being grateful and appreciative of what God has done. The commit is to worship and testify how and why God is so good to a person.

In conclusion, it is vital and imperative that having a relationship with Lord Jesus Christ will give a person assurance, confidence, and tranquility to know, believe, and trust that the Lord will fix anything in a person's life.

{Thought for the Week}
"I know the Lord will fix it for me."

Week 25

Surely, He Has Borne Our Griefs!

Isaiah 53:4-5
"Surely he hath borne our griefs, and carried our sorrows:
yet we did esteem him stricken, smitten of God, and afflicted.
But he was wounded for our transgressions,
he was bruised for our iniquities: the chastisement of our peace was upon him;
and with his stripes we are healed."
(KJV)

The scripture above is indicating that a person was given a promise from God about being healed and delivered from an individual's sins. There is a direct correlation between sins that is composed within **emotional, psychological, and spiritual hurts**. The truth of the matter is the Lord Almighty always provided a promise to be healed from those wounds and hurts. The Lord made a promise, which means that **healing and deliverance** has already been provided.

Through acknowledging and understanding a person hurts, the scripture states, *"Surely he hath borne our griefs, and carried our sorrows."* The word (*Surely*) means that **God has provided away to remove or take away a person's hurts**. The words **grief and sorrow** means that a person was hurting and dealing with pain. Pain is not just a physical ailment, but mostly, it is an emotional and psychological pain. Emotional and psychological pain is slow type of death, which bring **sorrow and grief very slow death**.

The truth of the matter is that Jesus Christ was a person's substitute to be crucified on Calvary's Cross. The scripture states, *"yet we did esteem him stricken, smitten of God, and afflicted."* The word **afflicted** means that Jesus Christ beaten or whipped for the individual. This is a praise break, because Jesus Christ became our substitute. He faced the **pain, misery, and agony of the cross**, so we wouldn't have gone to Calvary's Cross.

However, the cross was ultimate sacrifice for the remission of individual's sin. The phase, *"But he was wounded for our transgressions, he was bruised for our iniquities; the chastisement of our peace was upon him;"* The words **transgressions, iniquities, and chastisement** are keys words that indicates a person's sin was taken to the cross by Jesus Christ. It was Calvary's Cross that proves to a person that Jesus Christ came to take away his/her sins.

The blessings of these verses are found in the latter part of these verses, which is *"and with his stripes we are healed."* The phase is, *"his stripes we are healed."* This means that are healing have been already been done. The Calvary's Cross provided not only atonement for our sins, but the key is that God has given us a promised of being healed through and by the cross.

In conclusion, God has surely provided away for the individual to be saved, delivered, and rescued from sin. Through being rescued from sins, the Lord had provided healing from our **sins, because sin will cause hurt, misery, and pain.**

{Thought for the Week}
"The Lord had provided healing from our sins."

Week 26

O House of Aaron

Psalm 115:10
"O house of Aaron, trust in the Lord:
he is their help and their shield."
(KJV)

The scripture above is talking about the Lord's House. The Lord's House is the representation of the local assembly. The local assembly is where those who are saints (*believers*) come to *"worship, praise, fellowship, and commune"* with those of like faith. A person's faith growths when he/she is around those who have the same *"common interest and eagerness to grow within one's salvation."* Having Jesus Christ living and abiding on the inside, it is essential and imperative that a person should be drawn to others of like faith. It is through drawing to others that a person begins to establish and strengthen the individual inner man from within.

The phase *"O house of Aaron"* means *the church folks who are born-again and filled with the Holy Spirit.* The place in this phase, *"O house of Aaron"* have significant meaning and purpose. Aaron represents levities those who are called *"to be priest or worship leaders"* in the temple. It is important that the believer understands that those who are like the, *"House of Aaron"* are worshipers. Worshipers are those who come to the local assembly not only ready to worship God, but leading others into *"worship through teaching, preaching, and sharing God's word with others."*

The 1ˢᵗ thing is trust in the Lord. Psalm 115:10, *"O house of Aaron, trust in the Lord:"* It is through being a worshiper leader, a person learn how to trust in the Lord. Being in God's presence, it teaches and builds confidence within the individual. Learning to reply and depend on the Lord is a primary component to being a worshiper. A worshiper is a person who *leans, depends, and lives* by total faith in God.

The 2ⁿᵈ thing is knowing that the Lord will help. Psalm 115:10, *"he is their help"* The word help means *to aid, support, or assist*. A worshiper knows that God will come to his/her rescue when he/she truly comes on His name for help. The reason why the Lord runs to a worshiper side to help, aid, and assist, because a worshiper knows how to pull on heart of God to get response from Him. A believer must know that worship will summon God to help the worshiper.

The 3ʳᵈ and final thing is knowing that the Lord is a shield. Psalm 115:10, *"he is their help and their shield."* The word shield means to cover or protect. A worshiper realized and understand that God is protect and He knows how to cover a worshiper from attract of the enemy. The greatest defense to protect or cover a worshiper from attract of the enemy is worship. Through worship, a person will found out and discover that God is a shield. *Worship is designed to summon God to help and shield a person from any attack and provide security for the individual.*

In conclusion, the House of Aaron is those who are worship leaders that lead others into the presence of God.

{Thought for the Week}
"The House of Aaron are those who worship God."

Week 27

Nicodemus Needs To Know God

John 3:3
*"Jesus answered and said unto him, Verily, verily,
I say unto thee, Except a man be born again,
he cannot see the kingdom of God."*
(KJV)

Nicodemus is a familiar biblical story about a religious leader who has positions, titles, and status, but never been born-again and filled with the Holy Spirit. Nicodemus name in the Greek means, *"innocent blood"*, which indicates that his heart *is pure, genuine, and real*. There are sometimes people who are *holding positions, titles, and status within the church or community who are pure, genuine, and real, but do not have a relationship with the Lord*. Being good is not enough, because good people are not the qualification for being admitted into heaven. Heaven requirement is being born-again and filled with the Holy Spirit.

Salvation has become a lost message, because the church has moved to a *place, position, and mindset of thinking, believing, and understanding* of reaching the world by the world standards. The Nicodemus account in the Bible gives a person clear understanding that he/she must be *saved and be baptized in the Holy Spirit to be sealed with Heaven stamp and approval*. Heaven is a real place and it is prepared for prepared people. The change of a person heart and mind must be changed through the redemption power of Jesus Christ. It is only through accepting and receiving salvation that God changed a person *status, position, and place from hell to heaven bound*.

The 1st thing is accepting and receiving instruction from the Jesus Christ. John 3:3, *"Jesus answered and said unto him,"* Too accept and receive salvation, a person must hear and receive the message of salvation. It is only through hearing the word that a person can receive, but receiving is half of the message. Once a person receives the message of salvation, he/she must repent, believe, and turn to God and away from sin.

The 2nd thing is being opened to the truth. John 3:3, *"Verily, verily, I say unto thee,"* The phase verily, verily, is translated truly, truly. This means that a person must be real and truthful with him/herself. Truth is the only thing that a person must be willing to accept and receive about his/her self. The only way a person does not receive the truth, because he/she will allow *"self"*, which is fleshly nature that has not been crucified to keep him/her from accepting the truth.

The 3rd and final thing is change can only come when a person's eye is opened. John 3:3, *"Except a man be born again, he cannot see the kingdom of God."* Change can only occur when a person eyes is opened. Change can only happen when a person accepts and receives the reality of salvation, which causes a person's eyes to become opened. A person's eye is opened when a person sees God and his kingdom. The scripture states, *"Except a man be born again, he cannot see the kingdom of God."* The phase, *"be born again"*, which a person must be save and not act like he/

she is saved. There are a lot of people within the church circle are acting save, but he/she is not saved. It is important and essential that a person will "*be born-again*", which means he/she must live one's salvation out.

In conclusion, it is essential and imperative that an individual learn the lesson on Nicodemus conversation. The lesson is that Nicodemus was awake to the truth and he finally seen his "*self*", which indicated that he was lost without having a relationship with Jesus Christ.

{Thought for the Week}
"Nicodemus did not allow "*self*" to keep Him from receiving salvation."

Week 28

The Household of Faith

Galatians 6:10,
*"As we have therefore opportunity,
let us do good unto all men,
especially unto them who are of the household of faith."*
(KJV)

This lesson is about edifying each other within the body of Christ. It is essential and imperative the local assembly needs to know and learn the power of lifting and elevating each other. There is power, strength, and motivation that come from lifting up each other. Galatians 6:10, **"As we have therefore opportunity, let us do good unto all men, especially unto them who are of the household of faith." (KJV)**

The scripture stated **"…let us do good unto all men, especially unto them who are of the household of faith."** (KJV) The word let is interesting, because it means to permit or allow it to happen. It is not a forced or someone has to twist our arm, but it is willing to allow our kindness and love to flow out of our hearts towards those who are in the household of faith.

The Bible calls the church, **(…The Household of Faith)**. The church is the center and source for our faith to be **renewed, refueled, refined, reshaped, refreshed, revived, and restored**. It is imperative that we become a body of believers who is about edifying each other. This is the key and principle for keeping the purpose and substance within (Household of faith), which is the church.

The church is <u>*a body of baptized believers who are born-again and filled with the Holy Spirit.*</u> It should be objective of the church to meet this initiative, which is build up each other through aiding and guiding of Spirit of Christ. It is through His word, way, and will that we learn how to edify each other, so the Household of Faith can stay in line with God and purpose for the Lord establishing the Church, which is reaching and saving souls for Kingdom purpose and Eternal glory of God.

We are reminded and encouraged through word of God that we must do good to each other when there is an opportunity to do good to others. Galatians 6:10, *"As we have therefore opportunity, let us do good unto all men,.."* (KJV) The church as a whole can get rid of gossip, bitterness, anger, resentment, confusion, and other tools of emotional and psychological torment when we walk and live according to the word of God, which is to treat each other the way the Bible say treat each other. I John 4:18, *"**There is no fear in love; but perfect love casteth out fear: because fear hath torment. He that feareth is not made perfect in love.**"* (KJV)

In conclusion, it is important and essential to put our faith in God and God must be exemplify in His house so we can be called, **"The Household of Faith."**

{Thought for the Week}
"The Church must always be a Household of Faith."

Week 29

Lay Aside Every Weight

Hebrews 12:1
*"Wherefore seeing we also are compassed about with so great a cloud of witnesses,
let us lay aside every weight, and the sin which doth so easily beset us,
and let us run with patience the race that is set before us."*
(KJV)

What things are lurking in our hearts? Why do we allow idols become comfortable within our hearts? The answers to these questions are not simply or clear. It is essential and imperative that we remove useless things and objectives of destructive spiritual devices out of our hearts even when don't know how and why they are there.

These destructive spiritual devices are called "***weights that leads to sin***". Hebrews 12:1, **"…let us lay aside every weight, and the sin which doth so easily beset us, and let us run with patience the race that is set before us."** (KJV) The word weight from a theological and psychological point of view is referred as idols. These weights will cause sin and sin will lead to death and destructive spiritual devise, which will cause us to die spiritual and/or cause others to die spiritual.

There is sure thing about sin. Sin invades our lives with one intended plan and purpose, which is to promise death. James 1:15, **"…and sin, when it is finished, bringeth forth death."** (KJV) Reverend Eddie Salley Jr. stated, **"After death, there is no repentance, but judgment."** If we don't deal with sin that comes in our hearts through the form of idols, we will realize and understand that sin will cause death and no repentance will be needed, but judgment must take its place and result will be misery position and place for us.

Living a life that is full of idolatry is like living in vain. Vain living comes from pursuing and believing idols that lives in our hearts. Don't allow idols and prison of sin to cause us to live in vain. Matthew 16:26, **"For what is a man profited, if he shall gain the whole world, and lose his own soul? Or what shall a man give in exchange for his soul?"** (KJV) These questions are very thought provoking and penetrating, because there is a decision to make or not make to have a clean heart or a heart full of idols.

In conclusion, it is imperative a person learn and understand that remove idols from a person's heart is task that can be done by the person and asking help from God. However, he/she must make a commitment to lay aside those things that are not pleasing in the eyesight of God.

{Thought for the Week}
"Making a commitment to lay aside those things
that are not pleasing in God's eyesight."

Week 30

I Love the Lord

Psalm 116:1
"I Love the Lord,
because he hath heard my voice and
my supplication."
(KJV)

The scripture above is indicating and talking about a person whose have a relationship with the Lord Jesus Christ. Love is an action word that starts and lives within a person's heart. Love will cause a person to do good too those who are evil towards them. It speaks volumes of a real and sincere relationship that extends to those who the person comes in contract on a daily bases. No one can truly say that he/she love the Lord without have true authentic actions that follows those words.

The first thing is making a commitment to the Lord. Psalm 116:1, *"I Love the Lord,"* The essence of having a relationship with the Lord is personal relationship that has nothing to do with nobody else. No one can get this relationship with the Lord for an individual, because the individual must make up in his/her mind to make this commitment to the Lord. The word "I" is a personal commitment that derives from the individual's willingness, eagerness, and desire to have this relationship with God.

The second thing is having a reason to make a commitment to the Lord. Psalm 116:1, *"because he hath heard my voice and my supplication"*. It was the assurance of knowing that God will answer prayers. The victory of answer prayers come from having hope, faith, and belief that will ensure that your prayers are answered before they have been manifested. This is fuel that drives a person to continue to commit and commit to the Lord. Times will come that will try a person's faith and having a testimony that God can will ensure that victory and fuel patience to wait on the Lord.

The third and final thing is knowing that your are loving a real God. Psalms 116:1, *"because he hath heard my voice and my supplication"*. A real God will always love us back, because we love Him. The essence of answer prayers proves the point that God is real. The scripture states, *"Because he hath heard my voice and my supplication"* that indicates that God reveal himself to let us know that He is real. The Psalmist stated this word twice, *"my"*, which indicates that visitation of the Lord's presence made this reality become personal and intimate.

In conclusion, loving the Lord is making a personal statement without any reservation or doubt, because it derives from an intimate personal commitment that comes from personal experience of knowing that God is real.

{Thought for the Week}
"Loving the Lord is a personal intimate commitment."

Week 31

Adhering to the Lesson

Proverbs 8:33
"Hear instruction, and be wise,
and refuse it not."
(KJV)

When I am preparing a Bible Study lesson, I will always prepare a lesson with goals and objectives in mind to teach from. These goals and objectives will give me a format that comes with specific guidelines that I want the participants to receive and learn. A good lesson is best when a person learns how to follow the instruction, which simply means to obey the instructions of the lesson.

The first thing is to hear the instruction. Rules are mention to be followed, but a person must first hear the rules. Hearing is listening through understanding and comprehending what is being said. If a person does not hear the meaning and understand the meaning for a stop sign being in the neighbor, a wreck will soon occur, ticket will be written, or someone might get hurt, including one who is driving. It is important to hear the instructions, before acting on the instructions.

The second thing is be wise. The word wise means to exercise good judgment or use common sense in making a decision about a situation. There are some rules that are in place to help, assist, and support a person. However, it is important to have some common sense in carrying out those rules. No one can teach a person how to use his/her common sense, because he/she must learn that wisdom come from God. In order to be wise, it will take a longtime of experience of *"trial and error"* to gain wisdom to be wise in our planning, decisions, and actions.

The third and final thing is refuse it not. The refuse means to deny or not receive. It is important that a person will learn to receive and do not reject instruction. Rejecting instruction is like forget to take medicine when a person has a severe cold. The cold will only get worse, if a person rejects the truth about taking medicine. This is refusing instructions.

In conclusion, adhering to instruction is the key to understanding and learning to be wise. Wisdom will evidently come, if a person just waits on the Lord. Time has a way of teaching and showing a person that being wise is the key to following the instructions.

{Thought for the Week}
"The key to be wise is adhering to instructions."

Week 32

When God Loves Me

Proverbs 8:17
"I Love them that love me;
and those that seek me early shall find me."
(KJV)

The scripture is indicating a powerful truth about the character and nature of God. God's nature and character embodies love. ***He loves us so that He gave His Son to die, be buried, and finally, resurrected from a borrow grave to save us from our sins***. This is a shouting and praise break moment as we understand and embrace God's love. Embracing God's love is receiving His redemptive plan and purpose for our lives, which is to be restored back into fellowship with Him.

The first thing is God made His love a personal commitment to us. Proverbs 8:17, "*I Love them that love me;*" The word "*I*" means a personal commitment to us. It is appreciative and to be grateful that ***God's love is a personal commitment to us***. A personal commitment means a promise, which is agreement that God made with us. God is a God that does not lie, because His word is truth.

The second thing is that God promised of love is to those who love them. Proverbs 8:17, "*I Love them that love me;*" This is interesting statement in Bible that states, "*I Love them that love me;*" ***Too many times, we try to make the word say what it does not say***. The scripture is revealing that God does not love everybody. It is religious statement to say, "*I love everybody, because God said to love everybody.*" This is a lie, because it is virtually impossible to say, "I love everybody, because I know that no one love Bin Laden." The world was rejoicing that Bin Laden is die, which is indicating that we don't love Bin Laden.

The third and final thing is a condition to understand who God loves. Proverbs 8:17, "*and those that seek me early shall find me.*" God loves those who are willing to seek Him. A real and true Christian is those who are "***Seekers***". Seekers are those who seek God no matter what kind of challenges and obstacles come their way. Seekers are those who are willing to go through the storm and the rain. Seekers are those who are willing to go the extra mile when it seems that road had already ended.

Also, it is revealing of a promise to those who seek God. When we really seek God, we will find Him. It means that God will not hide himself from those who are seeking Him. This is why a sinner feels ascent from the Lord, because God is hidden from the sinner. The Bible teaches, "***no sinner can tarry in the presence of the Lord.***" The presence of Lord is always welcomes those who love Him.

In conclusion, love is nature and character of God and God's love makes and transforms our life to live and be like Him in the Earth. Anyone that does represent God's love is living outside of His protective and capable loving arms.

{Thoughts for the Week}
"God does not love everybody."

Week 33

The Lord Liveth

Psalm 18:46
"The Lord liveth; and blessed be my rock;
and let the God of my salvation be exalted."
(KJV)

The truth essence of Christianity is knowing that Jesus Christ is the living God. There are some religions that can't make this announcement about who they are serving. Jesus Christ had stated, "I am the resurrection and the life." This claim is about knowing that He lives and had never died. Why would we serve a God that is not real? How can we bow to a Savior who could not conqueror death, if we are planning to live again after we die? The answer to this question is yes, we can serve the Lord, because the Lord is a living God.

The first thing is the Lord Liveth. Psalm 18:46, *"The Lord liveth,"* The word *liveth* means to have movement, influence, and ability to more in strength and might. The phrase in this portion scripture states, *"The Lord liveth,"* The word Lord means Landlord. This is a phase that means He is the owner of everything. God owns life, death, pain, misery, and the list goes on and on. Because He owns all these things, He can have the legal right and authority to pronounce healing, life, and roll all our burdens away.

The second thing is the Lord is a rock. Psalm 18:46, *"and blessed be my rock;"* The word rock means a sure foundation or something that is huge and massive that can't be moved. The foundation of the Lord is sure and certainly it is blessed. The blessed means that God has favored and all source of blessings come from being on the rock. It is through holding and gripping onto the Rock, which is Jesus Christ. We are certain to become blessed.

The third and final thing is lift the name of God. Psalm 18:46, *"and let the God of my salvation be exalted."* The scripture that we should exalted the Lord, which means to give praise, glory, and honor too. All of our praise and glory goes the living God. He should be exalted (*lifted up*). He should be exalted (*praised up*). He should be exalted (*giving honor*) too. The reason why, because He gave us salvation that deliver, heal, and save us from horrible pits of sin, fallen angels, and the devil who blinded the eyes of them that lost. His name is worthy to be praised.

In conclusion, we serve a living God that lives within us. Just praise and magnify the Lord who is our living Savior.

{Thought for the Week}
"He is our living God."

Week 34

For the Commandment Is

Proverbs 6:23
"For the commandment is a lamp;
and the law is light;
and reproofs of instruction are the way of life:"
(KJV)

There is an old gospel song that states, *"I know the Lord will fix it for me."* Listening to this song, one of the verses tells the listener to, *"just live by His commandments."* The essence to being blessed is holding onto God's word, which is His commandment. A commandment is a rule or guidelines to govern by. The word truth of Bible is based governing and obeying His word, because His word works when it is obeyed.

The first thing is the commandment is a lamp. Proverbs 6:23, *"For the commandment is a lamp;"* The definition for the word lamp means *something that generates light, but deeper meaning is to illuminates the mind or soul*. The word comes not only to shine on things that were in the darkness, but bring clarity to a person mind and soul (*emotion, will, and reasoning*). Thank the Lord that He gave everybody His word to regulate our minds and souls.

The second thing is the commandment is light. Proverbs 6:23, *"For the commandment is a lamp; and the law is light;"* The word light means to bring awareness or reveal what is hidden in the dark. It is only through the law of God's word that a person was hiding in the safety of sin, which covered by image of darkness. When the word finds an individual, the word uncovers the individual and reveals to him/her the purpose, plan, and promise for walking in the light of the word.

The third and final thing is the commandments reproof with instruction. Proverbs 6:23, *"and reproofs of instruction are the way of life."* The reproofs means to correction, change, and make sufficient adjustments to a person behavior. The scripture stated a very interesting statement, which is *"reproofs of instruction."* It is through properly and timely correction that life comes into a person's life, because the word is correcting and changing the individual at the same time.

In conclusion, following the commandments are about holding and abiding by the truth of God's word. When a person abides by the truth,

{Thought for the Week}
"The commandment is the word and word brings all things to the light."

Week 35

The Man Behind The Words-Pt. 1

Mark 4:41
"And they feared exceedingly, and said one to another,
What manner of man is this,
that even the wind and the sea obey Him?
(KJV)

There is a cliché that states, "***Sticks and stones may break my bones, but words will never hurt me.***" This statement is false, because words have a way of hurting and cutting a person at the core of His or Her being. Words are so powerful and destructive that words can cause people to commit suicide, murder, and all kinds of sinful and hurtful acts. This is why the Bible teaches us about "***the power of life in death is in the tongue.***" The tongue with usage of the right words can destroy or strength a person.

In the above verse, Jesus Christ is using words or the power of words in the right place and at the right time. There are so many people lying in the bed of affliction, sitting in the jail house, or rioting in the graveyard, because a person had talked out of turn or said the wrong thing to cause that person to lose his or her life.

Jesus Christ is illustrating the proper usages of words in the above verse. The verse is indicating the power and authority that individual can speak to people, things, and places. God will honor and judge what a person speaks from his or her mouth. There is power and authority in the words that lies in a person inner man. The inner man is place of "***faith realm***" or "***where the Holy Spirit lives within the individual.***" With this understanding, words have a tendency not only form imagery in a person's mind, but words develop into life that comes from a seed (***word***) that grows within the individual.

When Jesus Christ spoke to the sea and wind, the word immediately had formed into life and caused the wind and sea to obey Him. ***Please understand that having authority is one thing, but using authority is another***. There are a lot of people who have authority, but don't know how to use their authority. Jesus Christ demonstrated the proper use of authority, because words should be used to create peace and remove crisis and chaos from a person's life. The opposite of chaos and turmoil is peace and celebration. ***<u>There is no celebration and peace when confusion, chaos, and misery are in the midst of a place, thing, or person</u>***.

In conclusion, it is important that a person learn and understand that authority is important, but using authority is more imperative to know and understand. Having a weapon in the hands of a person who do not know how to use it, a person is standing in a *dangerous place and position.*

{Thought for the Week}
"The authority of words comes from within a person's inner spirit."

Week 36

The Man Behind The Words-Pt. 2

Mark 4:41
*"And they feared exceedingly, and said one to another,
What manner of man is this,
that even the wind and the sea obey Him?*
(KJV)

The lesson in this scripture is indicating that things will cause a person to become fearful. Fear is stated in this way, *"False Enemy Appearing Real"*. This is a word phase to remember what fear can mean that fear is not real, but it is real. It gives us allusion that fear will transform images that are not real.

The definition of fear *is something that causes feelings of dread or apprehension and a distressing emotion aroused by impending danger, evil, pain, etc.* Fear has a way of gripping the soul, emotion, and mind individual that will cause him/her to succumb to evil of fear. The Bible teaches that *"God has not given a person a Spirit of Fear."*

It is extremely important to realize that God has not given a person a mindset or emotion of fear. Fear can only crump, walk, or talk it's way in a person's life, because a person has allowed fear to dominate and control his/her life. No who is a child of god should not walk, talk, or think in house filled of fear. The disciples had become fearful of the wind and sea. This is an interesting point, because wind and sea can be a destructive and deadly place and position to be in.

However, there are a lot of things that are in a person's life that is nothing, but wind and sea. *Don't allow the wind and sea of life cause you to fear*. Don't allow your emotions and minds to run wild and out of control, because wind and sea is trying to beat down your house. There is no reason to fear the wind and sea, if you are a born-again child of God, because God has given you authority to speak to wind and speak.

Speaking to wind and sea is possible when a person allows God to live in him/her. There is a songwriter that states, *"Live in me Jesus, have your way in me."* When God is having His way in you, you can stand up proclaim His word in the midst of a storm. When God is having His way in you, you can stand up speak to a chaotic atmosphere, the atmosphere will turn from chaos to peace. When God is having His way in you, *"the Spirit of the Holy Spirit will lift up a stand when the enemy rushes in on you like a flood."*

In conclusion, a person's lives in Jesus Christ and Jesus Christ in him/her. He/she does not allow wind and sea to dominate or control his/her environment or atmosphere. It is essential and imperative that a person learns to speak and walk in the authority of celebration of peace and victory that comes from Jesus Christ living and having His way, will, and word in a person's life.

{Thought for the Week}
"Don't allow your emotions and minds to run wild and out of control,
because wind and sea is trying to beat down your house."

Week 37

The Lord Will Be With You!

Joshua 1:9
"Have not I commanded thee?
Be strong and of a good courage; be not afraid,
neither be thou dismayed:
for the Lord thy God is with thee whithersoever thou goest."
(KJV)

The scripture above indicates that the Lord had given Joshua assurance and promise that He will be with him. ***A promise is vow or contractual agreement to specifically fulfill a requirement ot assignment.***. The Lord made a contract with Joshua, which is "*for the Lord thy God is with thee withersoever thou goest.*" This is encouragement to all of us who are "*trusting, obeying, and believing*" in the Lord God Almighty.

The first thing is being reminded of the promise. Joshua 1:9, "*Have not I commanded thee?*" This is a reminder that God has given us a commandment. This commandment is an oath, will, or instruction to perform God's will. It is important that when we are discourage and don't see a way out of no way. We must be reminded to revise the commandment and here the command that God will be with us. *The commandment serves as a reminder, but more importantly as an encourager.*

The second thing is hearing what God has placed in us. Joshua 1:9, "*Be strong and of a good courage*;" The Lord made us a promised, because He knows what He placed in us. The scripture indicated that the Lord had placed strength in us. When we know that we are strong, we can begin to take courage in the Lord. *Courage is the antidote to overcoming fear and discouragement.* This is why it is vital to know what God has invested in us and He is counting on us to fulfill and be those things that He placed in us.

The third thing is don't allow the wrong thoughts to remain in your mind. Joshua 1:9, "*be not afraid, neither be thou dismayed:*" Not only that the Lord will be with us, but we need to guard against discouragement and fear. There are some things that God wants us to *accomplish and do*, but fear and discouragement will cause us to avoid accomplishing those things. *Discouragement and fear is all in the same family when comes to keep us from being strong and of good courage.*

The fourth and final thing is knowing that God is with us. Joshua 1:9, "*for the Lord thy God is with thee whithersoever thou goest.*" There is a lot of encouragement in this phase, because the Lord states that He will be with us, but be with us everywhere we go. Not only is the Lord is walking with us, but He will continue to be with us no matter where we are. The Lord promised to be there with us and with us no matter where we go in this old life of ours.

In conclusion, it is important to know that God made promised and He does not forget or neglect to fulfill His promises.

{Though for the Week}
"God will always fulfill His promises."

Week 38

The Assurance of Praises

Psalm 18:3
"I will call upon the Lord, who is worthy to be praised:
so shall I be saved from mine enemies."
(KJV)

The scripture is talking about the assurance of praise. The word assurance means confident or certainty in one's ability. A praise is indicating that we know for sure that God is capable and able to act on our behalf. We praise God with this assurance, because He knows how to move and fix things in our lives.

The first thing is knowing who you are calling on. Psalm 18:3, *"I will call upon the Lord,"* To praise God, you must first know who you are praising (*calling on for help*). There are a lot of people praising God, but do not have a relationship with Him. The old fold will say, *"you have never been born-again and filled with the Holy Ghost."*

The misconception of about praise God (*everyone praising God*), because praising God is centered around having a relationship with the one you are calling on. If I don't know you, I will not answer nor pick up the phone when you call. The book of Life is the phone book, but you must be listed in the book so God's mind (***Caller I.D.***) will register you name, so He can respond to the call. To be registered in the Book of Life, a person must be born-again, which is to confess, repent, believe, and be saved from our sins.

The second thing is knowing the God deserves our praises. Psalm 18:3, *"who is worthy to be praised:"* **Every single day that we live, it is a day that we should give the Lord praises**. Praise is just tell God thank you for what you are doing and you are about to do. He deserves all of our praises, because He sent His only Son to die on the cross for our sin(s) so will have a choice not to face the penalty of sin, which is death.

The third and final thing is He promised to rescue me. Psalm 18:1, *"so shall I be saved from mine enemies."* Knowing that God will save us from our enemies is a promise and reason to give the Lord our praises. No one can't or should deny the fact that God is able to keep and deliver us from all evil and power of our enemies. **It is the devil's job to serve eviction notices on our lives, but the devil is not our Landlord**. The Lord Jesus Christ is our Landlord and we don't have to listen to cry of a false deity, but give praise to the real and true God.

In conclusion, the debate is not a debate, because praises will yield the assurance of the Lord making away for us. There is a songwriter that states, **"I know the Lord will make away somehow."** When you know the Lord will make a way for you, it should be given and second nature to praise the Lord.

{Thought for the Week}
"When the praises goes up, the blessings comes down
and this true results and assurances of praises."

Week 39

But I Will Maintain

Job 13:15
"Though he slay me, yet will I trust in him:
but I will maintain mine own ways before him."
(KJV)

The scripture above gives us insight on remain in the position and place with God no matter what condition we find ourselves in on life's journey. The journey of life will carry us through some pitfalls, downs, and many misery and pain. Yet, we called to keep our relationship with the Lord, because our condition and situation should move or stop us from **worshiping, fellowship, following, and communicating with our Lord and Savior**.

Job had interesting life, because he was man that went from riches to nothing and nothing to riches. His life is testimony and testament, because he understood that everything can lose and be destroyed, but he must keep his hand in the Lord's hand. There are some things that will cause us to grip onto God more or lose our grip. The choice is hang on or let go. The Apostle Paul stated, *"I will nothing separate me from the love of God."*

The first thing is understanding that we will have some bad days. Job 13:15, *"Though he slay me,"* The scripture states that God will slay me. The Lord will put us through some tests and trails. The tests and trails come to strength and better us, because trails and tests keep us focus on the Lord. This why James Cleveland wrote in song, *"God is not through with me yet. When God get through with me, I shall come forth as pure gold."*

The second thing is having yet in your "spirit" to continue to move forward with the Lord. Job 13:15, *"yet will I trust in him:"* The word yet means in the time still remaining. Job understood that God still have time to change his situation. In other words, he had yet praise inspite of his current condition. *A Yet Praise* is a praise for what my situation will be, because I know I still have time remaining. It is good to know that our time has not ended, but we still have time to praise and receive what God has for us. As a result, **A Yet Praise** is a praise of trusting God inspite of my situation. It is a praise that states, **"I will totally commit to the Lord no matter what my condition and situation states."** The scripture states, *"yet will I trust in him:"* **A Yet Praise** is a praise of total confidence and commitment to the Lord's will and trusting the fact that God knows what He is doing in my life no matter what the condition is.

The third and finally thing is keeping our standard before the Lord. Job 13:15, *"but I will maintain mine own ways before him."* The word maintains mean to keep at the same level or rate. My praise does not decrease, **it either maintain at the same level or increase beyond this** level. There are a lot of people who miss out on the blessings, because they do not keep at the same rate and pace. There is a word in the bible that states and confirms the meaning of maintain, which is faithfulness. The faithfulness means that a person must be consist and keep pace at the same level or except that level without decreasing. Faithfulness is having a maintain type of praise, which is **A Yet Praise**.

In conclusion, it is extremely vital that we understand that God blesses comes and flows in our life through consistency. Consistency is the key to maintaining and increasing our blessing through maintaining ***A Yet Praise***.

{Thought for the Week}
"It is important that we keep A Yet Praise in our soul."

Week 40

O Give Thanks Unto the Lord

Psalm 118:29
"O give thanks unto the Lord;
for he is good:
for his mercy endureth for ever."
(KJV)

The scripture of above indicates the true essence of gratitude (***giving thanks to the Lord***). Gratitude is showing appreciation with acts of humility for what someone has done for you. If the Lord has done anything for you, there should be act of humility through sowing and giving gratitude to the Lord for what He has done for you. When someone does something for you, the proper response is thank you. Being thankful or having an attitude of gratitude will indicate whether or not you have humility or humble for little or big things that God has done for you.

Gratitude is simply being thankful and appreciative what you are giving thanks for and about. When you are thankful, you are appreciative for big and little things that God has given to you. It is automatic utterance or act when you know that someone done something and you know that someone didn't have to do it. God has wakened you up this morning, but He didn't have to do it. A person should say, "***Thank You Lord.***" God has healed your body from time to time, but He didn't have to do it. A person should say, "***Thank You Lord for being a Healer.***"

The first thing is learning to give thanks unto the Lord. Psalm 118:29, *"O give thanks unto the Lord;"* It is imperative that a person learns to give thanks unto the Lord. The word give is key, because it is a volunteer act without anyone prompting you to do it. This type of appreciation must be within the individual before the individual gives a volunteer thanks or simply being humble enough to be appreciative for what God has done.

The second thing is knowing that the Lord is good. Psalm 118:29, *"for he is good:"* The word good is right, proper, or fit. When God does something for you, it right, proper, and fits. There is nothing that God does that is not right, proper, and fits. The reason why things are good for you, because you serves a good, (***right, proper, and fit***) God. The spouse you are married is right for you. The job you have, it fits you. The place you are going and being led by God is proper for you. All what God does for you; it is for your good.

The third and final thing is the Lord is merciful. Psalm 118:29, *"for his mercy endureth for ever."* The word mercy means to give divine favor or blessing. When the Lord is good to you, He gives a person divine favor and blessings. The blessings come, because God has favored you. You should be thankful and appreciative, because God has no only blessed you with blessings, but with divine favor.

In conclusion, the mark of appreciative individual is having divine favor and blessings following his/her life.

{Thought for the Week}
"The mark of appreciative person is having divine favor
and blessings flowing in his/her life."

Week 41

When Life Is Challenging

Romans 8:39
"Nor height, nor depth, nor any other creature,
shall be able to separate us from the love of God,
which is in Christ Jesus our Lord."
(KJV)

The above scripture gives us encouragement and hope to conqueror and handle life's challenges and circumstances. The word challenging means to, *"calling for full use of one's abilities or resources in a difficult but stimulating effort."* My practical definition is meeting the obstacle with assurance of victory, because you know the outcome do to having the Lord Jesus Christ on your side. **It is important to tap into the resources of our faith that will empower us to have the ability to meet the challenges in this ole world.** The truth of the matter is that all Christians suppose too be challenged, because a true and genuine Christian knows who handle and deal with challenges.

The first thing is don't be alarmed by the different types of challenges. Romans 8:39, *"Nor height, nor depth, nor any other creature"* The scripture indicates the different types of challenges. Some challenges will seem to be cumbersome and very measurable or deepness and intensity the situation maybe, because the Lord will sustain and give us the ability to carry us through.

Also, we will be able to overcome any creature, which means in this text means nothing in the Earth or under the Earth will be able to overcome us. Romans 8:39, *"No power in the sky above or in the earth below—indeed, nothing in all creation will ever be able to separate us from the love of God that is revealed in Christ Jesus our Lord."* (NLT) It is quite significant that God has given us hope and promise that the victory is already ours.

The second thing is having an unwavering commitment to the Lord Jesus Christ. Romans 8:39, *"shall be able to separate us from the love of God, which is in Christ Jesus our Lord."* The word separate means in the text, it is not take apart or undue a relationship. If you are really in love with Christ Jesus, there should be nothing that will cause a gulf or cause the relationship to be halted or altar. The scripture indicates that the love for Christ Jesus our Lord will cause and convince us not to allow anything to cause separation between our relationship with Christ Jesus.

The third and final thing is knowing the source to handling our challenges. Romans 8:39, *"shall be able to separate us from the love of God, which is in Christ Jesus our Lord."* Our source comes from the God and knowing Him as our Lord, which is accepting Jesus Christ as our Lord and Savior. The scripture made to reference about who God is. He is our Lord and He is our Savior (Christ Jesus). The source to overcoming life challenges knows who the Lord God is. He is the Creature and Landlord of everything that concerns us.

In conclusion, life will present all of us with creditable among of challenges, but knowing who the Lord Jesus Christ is and having a relationship with Him. He will strength and give us the resources and abilities to overcome those challenges.

{Thought for the Week}
"The life is a challenge, but it is no match for knowing and having
a relationship with the Lord Jesus Christ."

Week 42

Continue To Move Forward-Pt. 1

Philippians 3:13
"Brethren, I count not myself to have apprehended:
but this one thing I do, forgetting those things which are behind,
and reaching forth unto those things which are before,"
(KJV)

The above scripture is teaching about pressing and keep on moving those one's goals in life. There is slogan that states, *"Don't get struck on stupid."* Some people will themselves to *"get stuck on the stupid things"* of life and allow those things to stagnate and halt one's growth, which cause a person to stop moving forward. **One certainty about life, life does not stop moving, because a person is not willing to keep moving.** It behooves us to keep moving forward and continue to move forward no matter what a person circumstances states.

The first thing is don't get caught up in the middle of things. Philippians 3:13, *"Brethren, I count not myself to have apprehended:"* The word apprehended means to arrest of a crime, understand, or perceive. Paul is stating that he didn't allow himself to get caught up with things that tried make or found him guilty and shameful. It is those things that keep us from moving forward. To try to figure out why and how this had come to be, it is best to leave it in the hands of God and move on. There are some things a person should not try to figure out, because it beyond a person's *"pay grade."* This statement means, "it is out of our hands or control, but it is in the Lord Jesus Christ hands.

The second thing is knowing how to leave the pass in the pass. Philippians 3:13, *"but this one thing I do, forgetting those things which are behind,"* The key words in this portion of the verse are forgetting and behind. **There are some things a person needs to forget and put it behind him/her, because the pass is the pass.** Some people like to wonder and live in the pass, but pass is supposed to be the pass. This means, *"it is supposed to put aside and behind and the individual needs to move on."* Paul realized that the only thing that can keep him from moving forward is hanging, cleaving, and sticking to the pass. **The pass is meant to be behind and forgotten about, because it will hinder a person from moving on in the now and his/her tomorrow.**

The third and final thing is continue move forward towards one's aspirations and goals. Philippians 3:13, *"and reaching forth unto those things which are before,"* The key word in this portion of the verse is reaching. The word reaching mean to continue to strive for or always having a desire to accomplishes one's task. The worst thing a person can do is lose his/her desire and need to achieve. **The reason why, a person needs achievements, because it is small victories that enable and help a person to stay alive, motivate, and keep one's drive.** Without a drive within a person's spirit and soul, he/she will not ride or last a longtime in this Christian journey.

In conclusion, it is important that nothing and no one can stop a person's drive, unless one refuse to drive and take the ride no matter how short or long the trip is. A person must always keep moving forward.

{Thought for the Week}
"Without a drive within a person's spirit and soul,
he/she will not ride or last a longtime in this Christian journey."

Week 43

Continue To Move Forward-Pt. 2

Philippians 3:13
*"I press toward the mark for the prize of the high
calling of God in Christ Jesus."*
(KJV)

The scripture above is talking and encouraging a person to press his/her way through life's journey not matter what may come one's way. There is an ole Baptist hymn that is entitled, *"**I'm pressing on the upward way, New heights I'm gaining every day; Still praying as I onward bound, "Lord, plant my feet on higher ground.**"* This is the first line in this ole Baptist hymn, but the words give a person medicine for moving forward. The words talk about going upward, higher while you are praying, because Lord knows how to establish and settle you. The point is continuing to move forward.

The Paul is indicating one major factor in moving forward or continuing to move forward, which is pressing. The word pressing means some you are continuing to move and do no matter what. A person should always have a heart and mind to achieve, grow, and move on and beyond one's own circumstances and situations. **The disappointing thing is not what a press to move on, which is the enemy of progress.** When a person is not progressing, he/she is not moving.

The first thing a person must have is a commitment within to move forward. Philippians 3:14, *"I press toward the mark..."* The word *"I"* expressed an unwavering commitment that have emphasis on achieving and accomplishing one's task no matter what. A person must make a personal commitment to God and with him/herself not to waver or become halted in accomplishing one's own goals. This is very significant, because no one can stop, halt, or impede the process of growing and accomplishing one's dreams, inspirations, and goals, but the individual who made the commitment to capture those initiatives.

The second thing is knowing what you are trying to achieve. Philippians 3:14, *"I press toward the mark for the prize of the high calling of God in Christ Jesus."* No one is trying to accomplish or achieve a goal without knowing what a person is trying to capture. The verse indicates that **"I am pressing, because I am trying reach my prize."** A prize is something that gain and earned from mastering or fulfilling a particular assignment. There is not test that God does not bless a person for when he/she has truly accomplished and captured that prize. The prize within itself is the blessing, but blessing is not merely capturing the prize. It is knowing that God has given and ordained that a person becomes achievers and dream catchers.

The third thing is knowing that God has destiny you to do these things in His name. Philippians 3:14, *"I press toward the mark for the prize of the high calling of God in Christ Jesus."* One thing I have realized that God wants me to achieve and accomplish my goals, dreams, and aspirations. The key is to accomplishing those initiatives to do it with His ability and strength.

More importantly, God has called us to achieve, conqueror, seize, and overcome no matter what, because He is not a defeated God nor Savior. He is victorious and we are victorious in Him.

In conclusion, we should feel and empowered, because God has called, which means summon us to greatness.

{Thought for the Week}
"We are destined to be victorious."

Week 44

Opening the Door and Accept the Offer

Revelation 3:20
"Behold, I stand at the door, and knock:
if any man hear my voice, and open the door, I will come in to him,
and will sup with him, and he with me."
(KJV)

The scripture indicates that God is knocking at the door. The door in the Bible is representing opportunity and access to the blessings that God has for us. The key to receiving the blessing is opening the door and accepting the offer. The Lord has provided and made provision for us to be blessed, but the door must be opened by us to receive those blessings.

The first thing is recognize that God is at the door. Revelations 3:20, *"Behold, I stand at the door and knock;"* We must understand and realize that God is positioned and placed at the door. He is doing two things at the door, which are standing and knocking at the door. He is at door knocking. It is incumbent to hear, proceeds to the door, and open the door, unless we are just trying to ignore the knock and who at the door. To ignore the knock and who's at the door, it is to keep the blessing from flowing in our lives.

The second thing is listening to the voice at the door. Revelation 3:20, *"if any man hear my voice, and open the door, I will come in to him"* The purpose is receiving the blessings at the door comes from hearing the knock at the door. There are a lot of blessings come our way, but we are not listening and expecting those blessings. The key is revealed in verse to getting to the door to receive blessings, which is hearing God's voice. When we allow the world to desensitize our ears and minds, it is easy to not hear the voice at the door.

The third and final thing is allowing the Lord to come in. Revelations 3:20, *"and will sup with him, and he with me."* When the door is opened, God will come in sup and with us. This supping is called, *"fellowship, worship, and discipleship."* Through having *"fellowship, worship, and discipleship"*, this comes through having a relationship with the Lord and the Lord with us. God comes in with the plan, purpose, and promise to bless us with things, but most importantly establish and foster a true and meaningful relationship with the Lord.

In conclusion, it is important and essential that we must accept the offer at the door, because God is there knocking and waiting for us to answer.

{Thought for the Week}
"The knock at the door is the beginning of having a
meaningful relationship with the Lord,
but we must listen, open, and receive the blessing on the other side of the door."

Week 45

They That Are Sick-Pt. 1

Matthew 9:12
"But when Jesus heard that, he said unto them,
they that be whole need not a physician,
but they that are sick."
(KJV)

Have every visited a doctor's office? A Doctor office is a place where a person can receive all types of medical treatment and attention. Doctors are often one who always prescribes and writes prescribes for his/her patients that needs medicine for illnesses or aliments. It is important that a patient knows and understands that a doctor can help him/her in the time of need to help find solutions to his/her medical needs.

In the text, Jesus Christ is addressing and issue based on a question about being around sinners as the Pharisee had questioned Jesus Christ's disciples. Why the *"so called church folks"* are are always one questioning how Jesus Christ is ministering to sinners? How the church had came to a place to question whether or not Jesus Christ can minister to sinners?

The church has become so comfortable and complacent within his/herself that the church had lost the idea of ministering to those who are sinners. With this conclusion, the church has fallen into a place and condition of being sick. It is a sickness to question Jesus Christ on how and why He is ministering to the sinner. It is a sickness to have no understanding about the plan and purpose of the church.

Jesus Christ made a profound and fundamental true statement pertaining those who are lost. He stated, *"but they that are sick."* He addresses the individual, condition, and symptom all in one statement. He stated, *"but they that are sick."* **The word sick means to be affected by physical and mental illnesses.** A sick person's can by either physical or mental ailment, but it also can be both at the same time. Jesus Christ is addresses the mental sickness of the Pharisee (*religious rulers-church folks*), because they had lost touched with what the church is suppose to be all about.

In conclusion, it is extremely important that the church understand and willing to address the sickness within themselves before they try to address the sickness within others. Jesus Christ made a profound and relevant statement that needs to be discussed and addressed among those who suppose to be ministering to the lost, which is the body of Christ.

{Thought for the Week}
Does the church know that we have sickness within the body of Christ?

Week 46

They That Are Sick-Pt. 2

Matthew 9:12
*"But when Jesus heard that, he said unto them,
they that be whole need not a physician,
but they that are sick."*
(KJV)

What does it means to be sick? How does a person's seek help for his/her ailments and sickness? A person will unusually go to the doctor to get help for his/her medical attention. It is important that sickness occurs when a person is not willing or capable of address the ailment through some type of medical or psychological treatment. Often times, a person is walking around sick every day, but does not know, if he/she is sick or not.

The word sick means to be affected by physical and mental illnesses. In the definition, a sick person can have physical or mental illnesses or both. Jesus Christ is addressing the needs, desires, and wants of those who are identify as being sick. Jesus Christ had identifies those who are in need of a physician. He stated, ***"but they that are sick."*** He is addressing and cataloguing those who may have all types of conditions and symptoms. It is does not matter what your condition or ailment is. If a person is sick, the person is who Jesus Christ wants to bring wholeness to the individual's life.

It is important to realize and understand that ministries within any church should address and meet needs of those who are coming to church. All those who attend church should seek out to be whole and the church should be a place that a person can become and be whole. The verse stated, ***"they that be whole need not a physician,…"*** Being whole should be the objection, plan, and purpose for having ministries within any church that is preaching, teaching, and being an example of the gospel of Jesus Christ.

The whole means not broken, damage, or impaired, but intact. The purpose of church meaning the body of Christ is be in a position and place to mend those persons who comes through the doors of the local assembly. Broken vessels are seeking healed vessels to mend their brokenness within themselves. The verse stated, ***"they that be whole need not a physician, but they that are sick."*** The Lord Jesus Christ is always willing and able to mend those who are broken.

In conclusion, the issue of being whole had placed and positioned the church (***the born-again believer***) with the mindset, attitude, and genuine spirit of being whole, so the believer can effective and efficiently administer to those who are broken.

{Thought for the Week}
***"The church should be a place where all those who
come should experience the presence and be greeted with the spirit of wholeness."***

Week 47

My Issue for Twelve Years

Matthew 9:20-21
"And, Behold, a woman,
which was disease with an issue of blood twelve years,
came behind him, and touched the hem of his garment:
For she said within herself, If I may but touch his garment,
I shall be whole."
(KJV)

The Woman with the Issue of Blood is an interesting biblical story with a lot of truth in this parable. This woman had amazing ability to suffer-long and exercised a great deal of patience and wiliness to handle and deal with her issue. Her issue was a very severe illness that had blood for twelve long years. **The twelve long years is equivalent to 4, 383 days, 144 months, 624 weeks, and 105,192 hours.** The woman with issue of blood suffered long and had a lot of patience and diligence to preserve through those hard, touch, and consistent suffering without any end within sight.

This woman had issue that seem and look like it would not go away. Let us recapture the reality of her issue. **For twelve years, she blooded and suffered for 4, 383 days, 144 months, 624 weeks, and 105,192 hours.** It is even hard to image what this is like, because a small cold, four day flu, or sore ankle will make some of us throw in the towel. When people constantly talk about us for a few days, we are ready to give up. This woman had an unbelievable ability to over look the fault of her issue and see her need to be made whole. Can we see the need even when change is not in sight? Can we push and pull, until our change comes?

The first thing this woman did is kept believing that she could be healed.

The second thing this woman did is put her faith into action.

The third thing this woman did is press towards her breakthrough.

The fourth thing is this woman always expected to be made whole.

The fifth and final thing is this woman constantly reminds herself that she will be made whole.

No matter what her condition had stated and claimed to be at that moment, but she never fell victim to her circumstance. I heard Pastor Henry E. Dixon had stated in a sermon during a revival and he stated, *"Victory comes through toiling and toiling and not giving up."* This woman had understood the message of hope and promise, which is never giving up. This woman understood the message of overcoming, which is never giving up. This woman understood the message of defeating the odds, which is never giving up.

In conclusion, this woman had issue for twelve years, but she never gave up. The lesson in these verses tells us to move forward without allowing our issue to keep us down and move us backwards.

{Thought for the Week}
"Don't allow our issue keep us from having hope!"

Week 48

See What the Lord Has Done-Pt. 1

I Samuel 12:16
"Now therefore stand and see this great thing,
which the Lord will do before your eyes."
(KJV)

The scripture above is asking questions and making a statement about what God has done for us and will continue to do for us. It is a promise and commitment from the Lord and with the individual. When a person commitments to the Lord, the Lord will do marvelous in his/her sight. The question is simply, because a person needs to see what God has done and is doing in the person's life. Is God good to you sometimes or all the time? How many times has God rain down His blessings on you?

These questions may seem to be easy to answer, but someone does feel, think, and believe that God has done nothing or not enough for him/her. There is someone walking about thinking, believing, and feeling that there is no blessing(s) raining in his/her life. Some people may argue that God is not raining blessings, but misery in their lives. This is argumentative statement, but there is a lot of truth in these statements, because people are hurting, believing, and walking around thinking that all is lost and hope is not a reality for them.

How does a person combat these realities in their lives? Why is it important to see what the Lord has and is doing? These are very important and essential questions that will reveal the answer to a person's core beliefs, convictions, and issues. No one can answers these questions for anyone, but the individual must understand that most things occurs and happens to the individual, because one is taking a stand for something or not taking stand at all.

The first key is having and taking a position. The scripture states, *"Now therefore stand and see this great thing,…"* In order for God to move in a person's life, he/she must take position, which means have a standard and willing to stand in the right place to be blessed. There is one thing to take a position, but it is another thing to be in the right place and take the position. Reasons why things have fallen apart for people or (us) in particular, because we are not taking a stand or (having a standard to be blessed by God). God does not bless mess, but He brings us out the mess to bless us and remind us that we are anointed by our mess.

The second key is expecting to see great things. The scriptures states, *"Now therefore stand and see this great thing…"* The key word in this entire verse is *"Now."* It means at this particular moment and time, which is grasping and seizing the moment. This no time to waste, but wasting time comes from not seizing the moment. Stop looking at what is wrong, but learn to see what is great (*positive, productive, and amazing*). God is doing amazing things right now. He is not just doing them on tomorrow, next week, or next year, but He is doing great things right now.

In conclusion, it is important to stop and learning the value of having the Almighty God on our side. He is doing great things right now, but we must see those things.

{Thought for the Week}
Just stop and see what the Lord is doing right now!

Week 49

See What the Lord Has Done-Pt. 1

I Samuel 12:16
"Now therefore stand and see this great thing,
which the Lord will do before your eyes."
(KJV)

In the above scripture, it is indicating that hope is expected, because God is a God who delivers on all His promises. One main truth about assurety of God is that He does not lie. Lying is not in God's nature and character. The essence of serving, magnifying, and worshipping God is that He is truthful and real. This is why the scripture states, "They that worship me, must worship me in spirit and in truth." (John 4:24) Anybody can rest on the integrity of God's word, because His word is true, because He is a True and Living God.

Again, the word "**NOW**" is interesting statement in this verse, because it gives us hope to believe and receive the blessings that God has for us. The problem most people's spiritual and nature walk is that he/she does not expect anything, but failure. Failure in the sense has clouded and crowded a person's eyes with negative, discouragement, doubt, and fear. It is a strange thing to say that a person's believes in God, but don't have faith to expect God to help him/her with one's conditions, circumstances, and situations. The issue is that people don't trust and believe God.

The point of this verse is "**NOW**" means that we are willing to see what God is doing. I Samual 12:16, *"...and see this great thing,..."* The challenge for the individual is to see great thing(s). It is too often that a person is costumed to seeing bad things, but he/she needs to renew and conditional one mind and heart to see good things. There is a religious cliché that states, "The Lord is good and He is good all the time." This is a testimony of how a person views God and what God is doing for him/her.

Finally, the Lord is about doing His business, because the scripture states, *"...which the Lord will do before your eyes."* God is a God of fulfilling His promises, because He is always blessings His people. The scripture states, *"God rain of the just and the unjust."* (Matt. 5:45) The Lord does not hesitate to blessing His people, because He is in the blessing business. The one thing that prohibits and halters the blessing is not seeing what God is doing, which leads to doubt, fear, discouragement, and etc.

In conclusion, it is important to ask the Lord to open our eyes to see what He is doing, because God is just not up to something. But, He has already provided and released His promises of blessings to us.

{Thought for the Week}
"Just stop and look what God is doing,
but our eyes must be opened to see what He is doing."

Week 50

When I Believe In Jesus Christ-Pt. 1

John 9:38
"And he said, Lord, I believe. And he worshipped him."

The true indication of salvation is believing and then, acting on what a person's believes, knows, and feels. Salvation is both a feeling, knowing, and believing. However, the feeling is ignited by what the person knows and believes. There is too much errorous teaching about (soulish-emotional aspect of salvation) without placing the emotion into the proper context. It is hard to feel anything, if a person does not believe in it or believe that it is real.

Too much ministries are based on igniting soul, but not feeding soul to believe and know the will of God through the word of God. The souls of people are messed and mess over, because there is a lot of vain teaching and preaching that speaks to emotions, but never reaches the soul of the individual. The purpose of the word is to reach and penetrate the soul of the individual and not just tickle the emotions of the individual. The word is the only key component that will alien the soul (*emotion, will, and intellect*) with the will of God.

In essence, screaming, shouting, and dancing all around the temple (*church-born again believer*) building is good, but a person must measure the dance, scream, and shout from what have moved the individual to react in such away. The last I heard is "*heaven and earth will pass away, but the word will forever stand.*" As a result, the word is the key concept that places and position in a form of worship and releases a reaction for a person's soul. The release of reaction is from the soul being touched, stroked, and aroused by the word that provokes a dance, shout, or scream from the inner being of the soul.

The verse points out a significant view and understanding of believing in Jesus Christ, which is positioning and placing the individual in the realm of worship. Worship stems from a person believing in Jesus Christ as his/her Lord and Savior. No worship God without having accepted, believed, and confessed Jesus Christ as Lord and Savior, because it would not worship just vain worship that speaks to man and not God. The core of believing in Jesus Christ should provoke a response to worship God in the form that he/she knows and accepted God in personal relationship way that speaks and performance out of the depth of one's heart.

In conclusion, a person's believes in Jesus Christ through receiving the truth of God's word and the word touches the soul to provoke and proclaim a reaction to action of receiving God's word.

{Thought for the Week}
"If a person's believes in the Lord Jesus Christ,
it provokes a response of worshipping Him in truth and in spirit."

Week 51

When I Believe In Jesus Christ-Pt. 2

John 9:38
"And he said, Lord, I believe. And he worshipped him."

In the above scripture, it is indicating that worship proceeds only after a person's believes in Jesus Christ. Worship is how a person relates to God "*in spirit and in truth.*" The Spirit of God will lead and guide a person's into to place and position to worship God, but truth must accompany person going into to a place and position to worship God. It is impossible to attend to please God without faith, because faith is the key to ignite worship within the soul of the individual. (Heb. 11:6)

The word believe in this text is translated into the word faith, which means to believer or to trust in. The fundamental truth about worship, it takes an act of faith. No one can worship God without putting his/her trust in God. This is why the scripture is clear that a person's must worship God "*in spirit and in truth.*" (John 4:24) To have the accent of faith, it has accent of worship. If the person is not worshiping God with faith, his/her worship is mere exercising and natural flesh, which is sound brass and tinkling symbol. I Timothy 4:8, "*For bodily exercise profiteth little:...*"

The idea of worship should be done in faith, because faith resides in the center of one's will, emotion, and intent of one's heart. Faith is only thing that pleases God that provokes worship from depth of one's soul. The reason for exercising a person's faith during when worshiping God, because worship is *suppose to be personal and intimate and not just something to do.* It supposes to have meaning and purpose behind it and not just acting and exercising that produces little or no results. The absolute faith leads to the absolute worship of experiencing the true and living God.

Therefore, worship is having faith in Jesus Christ. No one can worship God without have connecting relationship with Jesus Christ through putting your trust in Him. This means a person must have accepted, believed, and received the gift of Holy Spirit. In other words, a person must be saved and filled with Holy Spirit. This seems to be an old fashion statement, but the truth is in God's word. John 9:38 states, "*And he said, Lord, I believe. And he worshipped him.*" Acceptance and receiving Jesus Christ is the key to having the right and access to worship God and not just be ungrateful, because a person can come boldly to the throne and attain mercy and grace in the time of need. (Hebrew 4:16)

In conclusion, no can escape the fact the salvation is essential to accessing the blessings of God that comes from a pure, true, genuine, and real worship. Worshiping God suppose and should be experience of emptying my soul and allowing a Holy God fill the person will His grace, mercy, and love.

{Thought for the Week}
"Worshiping God suppose and should be experience of emptying my soul and allowing a Holy God fill the person will His grace, mercy, and love."

Week 52

When I Believe In Jesus Christ-Pt. 3

John 9:38
"And he said, Lord, I believe. And he worshipped him."

In the above scripture, it is clear that worship without salvation is not worship at all. There are a lot of people who are thinking and believing that worship is place that a person assembly with others who have similar faith and belief. Worship is honoring, reverencing, and appreciating the God for Jesus Christ who died and rose again that all may have everlasting life. Worship is actually having the individual value his/her salvation with the Lord and Savior Jesus Christ. When a person's value his/her salvation, worship becomes a lifestyle and necessarily for living this Christian race.

The 1ˢᵗ thing is admit that you need Jesus Christ. John 9:38,"*And he said, Lord, I believe.....*" This is not just a statement of conversion, but admittance that the individual needs Jesus Christ. There are a lot of things that person does not need, but a person must have Jesus Christ to live in this world and to live again beyond this world into eternal. There is no escaping the truth of God's word that He will come back for the church that is "not spotted or winkled." If you have not admitted this truth, awful will be your condition.

The 2ⁿᵈ thing is believing in what you have admitted (confused}. *John 9:38, "And he said, Lord, I believe...."* There are a lot of false confession that individuals (all of us) have made, because individuals (all of us) have tried to appease the individual we are confessing too. Without believing in the confession, it is impossible to receive ransom for our sins. One thing about confession and believing in our confession as he/she must confess to God is and confess to Him is not appeasing, but being sincere. The Lord knows the individual hearts (intention, motives, or agenda), because He made the individual. There is no need to fake the confession, but believe in the confession.

The 3ʳᵈ and final thing is worshipping Jesus Christ. John 9:38, "*...and he worshipped him.*" The result of believing and confessing to Jesus Christ is worshipping Him. The sign of worship comes from a true confession and belief that the Lord Jesus Christ is real to the individual. There is no more praises to produces external display, but worship that is provoked and prompted by a confession and putting one faith in the Lord Jesus Christ. It is intimate connection that the soul is responding to change of salvation from the inside to the outside.

In conclusion, the act of worship comes from a deep abiding relationship with the Lord Jesus Christ. It is not external, but internal intimate relationship that individual and Lord Jesus Christ have with each other. Worship is more than conversation, but personal encounter with the Lord Jesus Christ.

{Thought for the Week}
"Worship is more than conversation, but personal encounter with the Lord Jesus Christ."

Do You Know Jesus Christ?

I hope and pray through your reading and studying in this devotional book that you have discovered and find comfort in developing and growing with the Lord Jesus Christ. However, if you don't know Christ, here is an opportunity to accept Him as your personal Savior or renew your relationship with him. Repeat this prayer!

Father in the name of Jesus Christ! I come to you with all my sins and burdens and I give them to you. I pray in the name of Jesus Christ that you will forgive me of my sins. Thank you for sending Jesus Christ to die on the cross in my place and cleanse me from all my sins. I ask you in Jesus name to come in my heart, mind, soul, and body and lead me into your divine will and way. I ask and confess you as my Savior and Lord and denounce Satan forever and forever. In Jesus Christ name, I pray, Amen!

If you prayed the prayer of faith, you are now saved and delivered from all your sins. Now, walk in the light of salvation and know, you are no longer under the bondage and condemnation of sin. Praise the Lord, Amen!

Sign your covenant agreement with Lord and Savior Jesus Christ.

Dear Jesus Christ,

I,_____ commit my life to my Lord and Savior Jesus Christ. I,_____ to walk, talk, and live truthful, sincerely, and honestly and allow the Holy Spirit to led in such away that your name will be glorified and honored. Thank you for accepting me into your Kingdom.

Sincerely Yours,

X_____

Special Note: Your next move is to join a local church that preaches, teaches, and be example of biblical truth, which practices and examples of God's word were you can continue to grow and flourish and allow the Lord to led you to that place of growth and development. **May God bless you in your Christian journey!**

Printed in the United States
By Bookmasters